A REBEL ACT

A REBEL ACT

MICHAEL HARTNETT'S
FAREWELL TO ENGLISH

PAT WALSH

MERCIER PRESS
IRISH PUBLISHER – IRISH STORY

MERCIER PRESS

Cork

www.mercierpress.ie

ISBN: 978 1 85635 967 2

10 9 8 7 6 5 4 3 2 1

A CIP record for this title is available from the British Library

Printed and bound in the EU.

CONTENTS

Acknowledgements

I would like to thank Patricia Corish, Sean Kehoe, Dympna Reilly and all my former colleagues in the Dun Laoghaire–Rathdown Public Library Service for their help.

Gratitude also to Hugh Comerford, Senior Librarian, and the staff of the Dublin City Library and Archives in Pearse Street.

The National Library, as ever, proved a valuable resource.

Pat Collins of Harvest Films, and Karen Wall and Gerard Sweeney of the Irish Film Institute were very accommodating.

Thanks also to the staff of Mercier Press.

Particular mention should be given to Rosemary Hartnett, Niall Hartnett and Lara Goulding for reading the manuscript and providing me with valuable information. Also to Peter Fallon of The Gallery Press, who kindly granted permission to reproduce the poems of Michael Hartnett in this publication.

INTRODUCTION

'My road towards Gaelic has been long and haphazard and, up to recently, a road travelled without purpose.'[1] So Michael Hartnett described it in an article in *The Irish Times* entitled 'Why Write in Irish?', explaining a decision that many of his friends thought unwise, to say the very least. At a poetry evening organised by Goldsmith Press on 4 June 1974, Michael Hartnett announced his intention to stop writing poetry in English from the stage of the Peacock Theatre in Dublin. After over a decade of publishing poems in 'the gravel of Anglo-Saxon', he declared that he was no longer going to do so. He was going to write in Irish from then on.

Hartnett had made his name as a poet in English but now he was to say goodbye to all that. He was one of the leading poets of his generation so it was a curious act of defiance, taking a vow of silence in the language in which he had developed his reputation. He intended to concentrate on Irish, a language which he could speak but not one in which he was overly fluent, not being a native Irish speaker. He was aware of the challenge he had set himself, and expected it would take him two or three years of study 'to sort myself out'.[2]

It was a momentous decision for a married man with two children to make. He was also about to take leave of absence from his job as a night telephonist in Dublin, but he had been thinking about it for quite a while. Hartnett felt it was time for a change; as he recalled many years later, with a certain ironic exaggeration, 'I sat down when I was thirty-three, the age Christ died ...'[3]

Hartnett had been concerned for some time about the future of the Irish language and he decided to do something about it. It was a flamboyant gesture, a symbolic act; a statement that language was important, that poetry was important and that he, Michael Hartnett, mattered. It was an act as much personal as political. Hartnett didn't expect any other writers to follow his lead. He was acting as an individual, not as the leader of a movement. But he was not going to go quietly. It was to be a public act of changed poetic allegiance, a grand theatrical gesture, no less sincere for all that. As he explained:

> I suppose I did solve, for myself, a problem besetting many poets writing in Ireland. I 'realised' my identity and came to terms with it … my going into Gaelic simplified things for me and gave me answers which may be naïve but at least give me somewhere to stand. The outline of my conclusion is as follows. There are Gaelic poets and there are Anglo-Irish poets.[4]

Hartnett had great admiration for the bards of ancient Ireland and the influence that they had had on their society. He yearned for such an influence but, in Ireland in the 1970s, he did not believe that poets were listened to or respected in the same way. He felt that poetry remained relevant even if it was overlooked in modern Ireland. As he put it, 'You see, poetry is no longer necessary but poets still exist.'[5]

His announcement, in June 1974, created barely a ripple, except in literary circles. Hartnett composed a poem called 'A Farewell to English', which gave the background that led to his decision. Fellow poet Brendan Kennelly had advised Hartnett that if he was going to quit writing in English he should do it in style. Hartnett actually dedicated the finished poem to Kennelly. It was published in 1975, in a collection with the same title, in which he expanded on his gesture of renunciation. It was not enough just to write in Irish, he must write in Irish at the expense of writing in English.

Part dream sequence, part satire, it was polemical in nature. The poet even says his goodbyes to the poets he had read in translation, Lorca and Pasternak:

> I say farewell to English verse
> to those I found in English nets:
> my Lorca holding out his arms
> to love the beauty of his bullets,
> Pasternak who outlived Stalin
> and died because of lesser beasts:[6]

To return to his mother tongue he must leave these behind.

In Hartnett's *A Farewell to English*, W. B. Yeats comes in for specific criticism, as much for his influence as for his deeds:

> Chef Yeats, that master of the use of herbs
> could raise mere stew to a glorious height,[7]

Later in the poem he states:

> For Gaelic is our final sign that
> we are human, therefore not a herd.[8]

According to Hartnett, English for him was 'the perfect language to sell pigs in'. Hartnett believed that writers had a responsibility and an influence beyond the merely literary:

> Poets with progress
> make no peace or pact:

the act of poetry
is a rebel act.[9]

Hartnett concluded with a final affirmation:

I have made my choice
and leave with little weeping:
I have come with meagre voice
to court the language of my people.[10]

1

'1941 WAS A TERRIBLE YEAR'

Michael Hartnett was born in Croom Hospital, County Limerick, in 1941, into an English-speaking small-town, working-class family. His parents, Denis and Bridie Harnett, lived in Newcastle West. As he put it himself, not entirely seriously:

> Nineteen forty-one was a terrible year
> The bread it was black and the butter was dear[1]

Food rationing during the Second World War affected even rural Limerick, especially in a poverty-stricken family like the Harnetts:

> And to cap it all off I appeared on the scene
> And threw everything into disorder[2]

Right from the beginning there was an element of duality in him. 'His birth certificate incorrectly entered the name Hartnett, as opposed to Harnett, but Michael was later reluctant to change it back because he felt that Hartnett was closer to the Irish Ó hAirtnéide ...'[3] In fact, for the early part of his life and career he went by the name Michael Harnett, and his initial works were published under this surname.

Michael was the eldest child. Within the next few years he was joined by four brothers and a sister: William, Mary, Denis, Gerard and John. Two other siblings died while young: Edward

11

was born on 12 October 1942 and died on 29 November 1942; Patricia lived for three years.

Michael himself was a sickly child and spent his first week in Croom Hospital. It was felt that 'there was no chance that I'd survive at all'.[4] But survive he did. 'My Ma fed me goody and milk from a spoon,' he said in 'Maiden Street Ballad' many years later.

The young family lived in rented premises on Connolly Terrace in Newcastle West, then on Church Street and eventually they moved to 'a mansion' on Lower Maiden Street 'because we wanted to live among the elite'. Their landlord was Legsa Murphy and the rent was three shillings a week. The 'mansion's' walls were made of mud and the roof leaked. As Hartnett described in 'Maiden Street Ballad', 'our mice nearly died of starvation'.

Times were hard and he was fostered out to his relations. For much of his early life he was brought up by his grandmother Brigid Halpin, who lived in the townland of Camas in Temple-glantine. In contrast to the urban life in small-town Newcastle West, where he was a 'townie born and bred', his grandmother lived on a rural farm.[5] It was a momentous change for him; a window into a different world.

My first contact with Gaelic as a living language was in 1945 when I went to stay with my grandmother. She was a native speaker and had been born in North Kerry in the 1880s. She rarely used Gaelic for conversation purposes but a good fifty per cent of her vocabulary was Gaelic – more especially those words for plants, birds, farm implements, etc. She occasionally sang a Gaelic song. I was not aware of anything unusual in the mixing of languages but simply absorbed the words without question and used them in normal conversation. I learned some two thousand words and phrases from her.[6]

Hartnett described in later life how Brigid Halpin showed him 'the harp side of the Irish coin'. She did not speak Irish to her immediate family but she did with her cronies. While they were playing cards at night, Hartnett would be up in the loft in his bed listening to the banter. He learned Irish by osmosis and, in fact, did not differentiate between Irish and English until he went to school and found out that they were, in fact, two different languages.[7] To Hartnett she was a very Gaelic nineteenth-century woman; a woman out of time. She never came to terms with the twentieth century. 'Television, radio, electricity were beyond her ken entirely.'[8] He took great pride in her.

> I remember with joy for myself, my grandmother coming into town on her ass-cart, her black-fringed shawl about her small fresh face, with her story of pishogues and enchanted fairy-forts. I remember her dancing on the road to a comb-and-paper hornpipe.[9]

She ventured into Newcastle West on pension day, 'in a flurry of hat-pins, with her shawl wrapped around'.

However, he was not blinkered about the life Brigid Halpin led. She was no angel:

> All the perversions of the soul
> I learnt on a small farm,
> how to do the neighbours harm
> by magic, how to hate.
> I was abandoned to their tragedies,
> minor but unyielding.[10]

As a young boy, while staying in the country in Camas with his grandmother, an incident occurred that made a major impression on him. He was playing outside the house when a bunch of wrens surrounded him. He ran into the kitchen and told Brigid Halpin, 'Granny all the baby wrens landed on my chest.' She said to him in English, 'You're going to be a poet.' He was six or seven at the time. Despite this, he didn't write a word of poetry until he was fourteen or fifteen.[11] However, from an early age he had shown an interest in books.

> My father was a very well-read man. There were always books in the house. My grandmother on my mother's side was also well read. I was reared on a dose of ballads and Canon Sheehan's novels ... So I was very much aware of literature. I joined the Newcastle West library in 1945, when I was four years old. I was able to read then.[12]

In those days he often tried to read by the faint light of an old oil lamp which was suspended from the rafters.

> The house seemed big at the time but is really incredibly small, and one had to stoop to enter. I sat there in the small kitchen-cum-living-room, innocently working out the problems my father set me. 'If it took a beetle a week to walk a fortnight, how long would it take two drunken soldiers to swim out of a barrel of treacle?' I never worked it out. Or, 'how would you get from the top of Church Street to the end of Bridge Street without passing a pub?' He did supply the answer to that, which indeed is the logical answer for any Irishman. 'You don't pass any – you go into them all.'[13]

Hartnett was a solitary child: 'I was very much a loner ... I have brothers and sisters but I hardly knew them when I was young'.[14] It is not clear when he moved back to Newcastle West but it may have been when he was due to start school.

Newcastle West was a small town. There was not much in the way of luxury, not in Maiden Street at any rate.

In the early days for the All-Ireland final they used to place the one radio in the town on the window of a local pub so all the people could hear the match. Of course, the more important people got to sit close to the radio. Michael said he never heard a word of the commentary.[15]

Newcastle West had a certain wry image of itself, reflected in the local saying: 'Church Street without a church, Bishop Street without a bishop and Maiden Street without a maiden'.[16]

From Hartnett's own description Maiden Street was little more than a slum. 'The street was mainly a double row of mudhouses, some thatched, a few slated, most covered in sheets of corrugated iron. This was Lower Maiden Street. Upper Maiden Street was given over to small shops and public houses.'[17] Hartnett compared it to the Claddagh in Galway city: 'It was one of those remnants of those depressed areas to be found in every city and garrison town such as the many "Liberties" and "Irishtowns".'[18]

As a working-class 'townie', Hartnett was acutely aware of a pecking order in Newcastle West. He recalled one illuminating occasion when he took a young friend home to Maiden Street: 'Please don't tell my father I'm down here,' the ten-year-old boy said. 'The town was small and he had never been "down there" before nor was he allowed go down there by his parents.'

There was a shocking level of deprivation in the area. Tea chests, flour bags and jam jars had a secondary use as household items: tea chests served as cradles and playpens; jam jars were a poor man's china. To drink hot tea from a jam jar demanded great skill, as did the filling of it. First, the milk and sugar were put in, to avoid splitting the glass, then the tea to the very top. It had to be stirred very gently. It was not held in the hands at first, but laid on the table in front of the diner, who sucked at the top. By the time the tea had gone down too far to be sucked, the jar was usually cool enough to be handled.[19]

Religion played a large part in public life. Hartnett recalled how before the Corpus Christi procession every year:

> all walls were lime-washed in bright yellow, red and white colours, windows were aglow with candles and garish statues and any unsightly object such as a telegraph pole, was garlanded in ivy or ash branches. Banners and bunting spread across the houses and on the day with the ragged brass band blowing brass hymns followed by all the townspeople who carried confraternity staffs, the Host under a gold canopy was carried through the town. It matched any *Semana Santa* procession in Spain.[20]

As he put it in 'Maiden Street Ballad', the band made up in enthusiasm what it may have lacked in quality:

> I remember quite well the Confraternity Band
> in the procession they sounded so grand
> the front they played one tune while in the back rank
> they struggled with 'Faith of our Fathers'.[21]

Some old country customs had survived in the town, though Hartnett was acutely aware that the life into which he was born was fading away. He recalled playing 'Skeilg' once a year, 'chasing unmarried girls with ropes through the street, threatening to take them to Sceilig Mhichíl'. Bonfire Night was still celebrated.

Another pastime was putting pebbles in a *toisin* (a twisted cone of paper in which shopkeepers served sweets) and leaving it on the street. If anyone picked it up and opened it, the person who left it would lose his warts, one for each pebble in the paper, and the person who picked up the paper took the warts.[22]

There were still vestiges of other folk traditions where the source of the original tradition had been forgotten. 'The ritual lighting of bone-fires (bones were originally used) on St John's Eve still went on in the 1940s and 1950s but we did not know why … it was a custom without a heart, without a reason.'[23] Many of the customs were slowly dying as Hartnett grew up in the 1950s. 'We had a town crier (called locally the bell-man) in Newcastle West, up to 1960 …'[24]

Maiden Street's 'houses were small and with no sanitation. One fountain served the whole street.' There was no electricity either. 'Candles and paraffin lamps did not brighten the darkness in kitchens on Maiden Street – they only made the gloom amber.'[25] The houses had mud floors and large open hearths with cranes and pothooks to take the cast-iron pots. Most of the small houses contained very large families. In 1948, the Coalition government started work on a housing estate on a hill overlooking Maiden Street. By 1951, the estate was finished, and many of the residents of Maiden Street went there, including the Harnett family, who moved into 28 Assumpta Park on 13 September 1951. Even in later life Hartnett remembered the exact date. It was the first time that he could read or write by electricity.[26] The new houses had, as Hartnett put it, 'toilets and taps (six, I counted, overjoyed), electricity and upstairs bedrooms. But Skeilg was never played again.'[27]

One of the family's first acquisitions was a Bush radio. 'And so from the ages of ten to nineteen I had access to music, Irish, pop and classical; to *The Goon Show* and to Austin Clarke's poetry pro-grammes.'[28] A whole new world had opened up for the ten-year-old boy, and yet some of the old games continued. Pitch and toss 'was a pleasant sight to see, men and boys on a summer's evening, cursing and swearing over a few pence in the dirt, or running like hell from the guards'.[29]

Not every entertainment was as innocent; some were not without a touch of unkindness:

> watching crawfish clawing their way towards the river across the roadway, gambling with passing cars. And on hot dusty summer evenings (all the evenings of summers before adulthood seem hot and dusty) suddenly at the pub not far from our door, there would be the joyous sound of curses and breaking glass – joyous to us because we knew the tinkers were settling some family problem in their own way.

Such an event was akin to a spectator sport:

> We would sit on the window-sills, eating our rawked apples, while they fought. We never cheered, nor would any of those who appeared over the half doors up along the street. Someone would send for the gardaí, and then light carts and swift horses would rattle off down towards the Cork road, all the fighters friends before the common enemy. We sat on, waiting for the last act, when, half-an-hour later, the fat, amiable garda would come strolling down, to an outburst of non-malicious jeers. But we were poor too, and there was the misery of drink in many houses.

Christmas was particularly memorable:

> A shouting farmer with a shotgun, a few patch-trousered urchins,

soaked, snotty and unrepentant, running across wet fields, arms full of holly. The long walk on the railway tracks, the sleepers treacherous and slimy, the dark stations, the lamp-posts with their glittering circular rainbows. We stopped at the shops' red windows to admire toys we could never have. A few drunks waltzed by, happy and moronic. An open lorry went by to jeers and obscenities; the pluckers shawled and snuff-nosed on the back, on their way to a flea-filled poultry-store to pluck turkeys at nine-pence a head.[30]

Hartnett felt little in the way of nostalgia for these times as there was too much deprivation and hardship. Nor had he any time for the snobbery of his so-called betters:

The purloined holly hung on holy pictures. There were no balloons, no paper chains, no Christmas trees. Coal was bought by the half-stone, butter by the quarter-pound and tea by the half-ounce. The country people trotted by on donkey-and-cart or pony-and-trap with the 'Christmas' stones of sugar, pounds of tea. Women in shawls and second-hand coats from America stood at half-doors, their credit exhausted, while the spectre of Santa Claus loomed malevolently over the slates and thatch. Members of charitable institutions distributed turf and boots, God-blessing the meagre kitchens, as hated as the rent-man. They stood well-dressed on the stone floors, were sirred and doffed at. They paid their workers slave wages. They looked without pity at the nailed together chairs, the worn oil-cloth topped tables, the dead fires.[31]

Though not particularly pious himself, Hartnett appreciated the theatrical aspect of the religious celebrations:

Outside, the rain fell and blew along the street. The tinkers fought. Bonfires died out in the drizzle. We were washed and put to bed, happy and undernourished. The oldest went to midnight mass. The

Latin was magic, the organ, the big choir. It always seemed like a romantic time to die.

It was a Christmas of tin soldiers, tin aeroplanes and cardboard gimcracks. We were Cisco, Batman, Johnny Mack Brown all that day. Our presents – 'purties' we called them – seldom lasted longer than that day. It never snowed. There was no turkey, no plum pudding, no mince-pies. The Victorian Christmas was not yet compulsory. The very poor managed roast meat, usually mutton. We often rose to two cocks. The goose was common. There was fruit-cake, jelly and custard; the dinner of the year. I never remember drink being in the house. There were never visitors, nor were we encouraged to visit anyone. If the day had been anyway fine, we were to be found on the footpath or in the puddles, knuckles blue.[32]

If Christmas Day was spent at home, St Stephen's Day – the Wren's Day – was more sociable.

One fine frosty morning the sound sleep of our house, after the excess and boredom of Christmas Day, was magically finished by the excitement of bodhrán and the tin-whistles of a group of 'Wran-boys' from Castlemahon. I saw the masks and the weird costumes and was out of bed, searching my pockets for the pence of Christmas Day.

The Wran, the Wran, the king of all birds,
St Stephen's Day he was caught in the furze
Up with the kettle and down with the pan,
And give us a penny to bury the Wran.

Hartnett recalled the first and last time he saw a dead wren, complete with nest, held up in a furze bush, hung with red streamers. It was 1949, when he was eight years old:

The pubs were open on that day, and melodeons, pipes, bodhrán, fiddles, drums and tenor voices raced up and down the streets until night. It was like that for a few years …

The Wren's Day always brought frost. Small warm heads came from under rough blankets to the sound of flutes, banjos and bodhráns far up the street. We donned boot-polish and lipstick and old dresses and went out to follow the wren, tune-less chancers. We sang and giggled our way to a few bob and a glass of lemonade. The back kitchens of the pubs filled up with musicians, the musicians filled up with porter and their wives filled up with apprehension. In a few hours, winter took over again.[33]

However, in 1951, when the 'New Houses' were opened 'progress stepped in'. The Wran Boys still kept to the town but 'all we got was a few guitars and little boys with lipstick singing "I'm all shook up" or some such transient ditty'.[34] Hartnett regretted the passing of such traditions: 'better standards of living may improve the health of people, but this price of abandoning poor peoples' customs must always be paid and the customless bourgeoisie come into existence'. He feared that over time Newcastle West was becoming 'televisioned, educated and more middle-class every year. Is Dickie Rock to replace the Wren-Boy?'[35]

Nevertheless, years later, in 1984, when Hartnett wrote of the past in the *Old Limerick Journal*, there was no warm nostalgia for those good old days of poverty and deprivation. He concluded his reminiscences with the heartfelt wish, 'There will never the Christmases like those again, I hope to God.'[36]

Hartnett remembered that there was always music in his house. 'My father was a great singer. I should say he wasn't a great singer but he sang a lot.' Hartnett wasn't immune to the attractions of modern music either:

> I discovered Elvis Presley when I was 16 or 17 ... Buddy Holly and all that ... There were ceilis in the town ... the mixture was extraordinary ... there were no divisions ... Someone would get up and sing an Irish song. Then someone would sing an Elvis song 'I was stung by a sweet honey bee'. Nobody took objection.[37]

In Newcastle West, at the time, Hartnett felt there was no separation between the old Irish traditions and those of the modern world; there was an amalgamation between them.

In 1955, Hartnett spent a month in Cúil Aodha, where he spoke Irish all the time; his first contact with it as a social language. It had a strong effect on him while he was there: 'I began to think in Gaelic, to dream in it, and even, as I was told, to speak it in my sleep.'[38]

2

'LOOK WHAT HE WROTE FOR ME'

Despite his grandmother's forecast that he would be a poet, Hartnett did not take an interest in Irish literature until he was thirteen. He was unaware of the Gaelic heritage of the West Limerick area where he was raised:

> Like many Irish children I was reared on a diet of folktale, Republicanism and mediocre ballads. I knew some Gaelic but it was merely another school subject, not a key to another culture. But, in 1954, a friend, Seán Brouder told me of Ó Bruadair. He recited some verses, which he translated for me. He claimed that the poet had been born in my own town and had lived most of his life in my own county. I was enthralled. I knew what poets looked like from their portraits in library books, so I invented my own picture of Ó Bruadair. The following year I wrote and published my first poem – in English.[1]

Even though he had not read a word of Ó Bruadair, the poet had become for Hartnett a symbol of what he wanted to be. He was later disappointed to discover that, in all probability Ó Bruadair had not, in fact, been born in Newcastle West, although he had lived much of his life in West Limerick. Later, when he read his work, Hartnett was further disconcerted. He could not understand his verse; a 'gnarled, concertina'd kind of Gaelic written for a distant and savage people'. Modern poets such as Hopkins, Yeats and Eliot were more accessible.

By this time, while still at national school, he had begun to write poetry. As he recalled: 'In 1955 I wrote a very bad piece of verse which was published in the *Limerick Weekly Echo* ... I wrote the piece for no good reason, unless it were to make up for my poverty'.[2] This precocious act of creativity was to get him into difficulty:

> One of my teachers descended on me wrathfully. 'It was the work of that great poet T. D. Shanahan,' he said. The headmaster Frank Finucane defended me. The other teacher challenged me to write a set poem in two weeks. Frank Finucane called his class to a halt and with his encouragement I finished the poem in ten minutes. The other teacher retreated and never spoke to me again.[3]

The national school, which had been built in 1876, was in poor condition. 'It was unbelievable. In the summer the swallows built in the large beams inside the rooms, flying in and out all day to feed their young.'[4] One of his favourite pastimes was:

> drowning woodlice in the inkwells as they fell from the rafters ... Some of the boys who did not live in the town brought their lunches – bread and butter and milk – wrapped in newspaper, and these were raided almost every day by the rats who lived under the floor and scampered about ... Rat poison was put down and the entire school was pervaded in the delightful aroma of decaying rats.[5]

Hartnett left the national school in 1956 and as he put it 'lost an ally':

Secondary school came then and I wrote many poems (all fortunately lost) and made a new enemy, my English teacher … For five years I was beaten more often for 'meditating the Muse' as he called it, than for lack of learning.[6]

But writing did have its compensations: 'I did feel a bit strange sometimes when I would go away, avoid everybody and start writing. I was wondering why everybody wasn't doing it.'

Hartnett wrote poems for the girls on demand in the secondary school to impress them: 'Look what he wrote for me.'[7]

In later years, Hartnett was dismissive of what he had written, 'small school-boy lyrics' he called them. As adolescence set in he felt that he was an isolated figure in Newcastle West, but the local library had Yeats and Hopkins to represent what was, to him, a link to the world of modern poetry. Another link was Austin Clarke's long-running poetry programme on Radio Éireann.[8] In later life, Hartnett recalled how he used listen to Clarke's monotone:

And I was back beside the Bush radio, the family creating their usual chaos, my mother ironing and saying: 'For God's sake will you turn off that droning!' And my father, mellow for the moment, after a few pints, saying 'Ah, let him alone.'[9]

The programmes introduced Hartnett to a whole gallery of poets, Irish and international, '… spoken by a low-register, sometimes harsh voice … The content … was eclectic.'

Life in Newcastle West could be difficult.

Any oppression I encountered was not direct, I was oppressed by what was inherent in the town's way of life, the patronising society that doled out bread and boots to the poor, the reading of subscriptions from the pulpit, the quashed scandals, dark secrets about the 'Troubles' and I was a poor man's son in a secondary school, a place I had no right to be, as I was often reminded.[10]

In 'Maiden Street Ballad' he made his own comments on these attitudes:

> There were shopkeepers there quite safe and secure,
> Seven masses a week and shit on the poor.
>
> They thought themselves better than their fellow man
> Now the nettles grow thick on their gravestones.[11]

In an article in 1969, in *The Irish Times*, he recalled:

> Once a year the otherwise idyllic life of the town was ruined by the coming of the 'Mission'. It was as if the Grand Inquisitor himself walked through the town pointing out heretics. I sat in the church on the long seats, sweating with fear at the Hell conjured up by the preaching father.

The priest threw:

> all sorts of vile accusations at the people. They sat, silent and red-eared, until he told an ancient joke, probably first told by Paul in Asia Minor, a joke that they had heard year in, year out, for a long time. But they tittered hysterically, delighted at being able to make a human sound in church. Outside, the 'Stalls', with its cheap trinkets from Japan, was dutifully looked over by the congregation, phials of Lourdes water, miraculous medals, scapulars, prayer-books and all the

tokens of religion bought and sold like fish-and-chips. But they were not 'holy' then, not until the end of the Mission did the preacher bless the huckster's dross and only then did they become sacred.[12]

The sexes had separate Missions: Men's Weekly and Women's Weekly. As Hartnett wryly reported, 'their sins, I assumed then, were different'.

Part of the old castle grounds had been made public by the Earl of Devon. 'These overgrown acres were a retreat from the Mission for anyone daring to go there during a service. Getting to the demesne from the town without having been seen was an art in itself.'[13] In fact, when Hartnett wrote about it a number of years later, he declared that he would not divulge the method of getting into the Demesne 'lest some young person read this and be led astray'. But once inside, 'it was a haven of quiet trees and overgrown paths and two rivers'. Hartnett read much poetry on such nights, while around him the area was alive with other refugees from the Mission. He recalled 'watching the shadowy figures of fellow transgressors hiding in the bushes, a small cloud of blue cigarette smoke over their heads'.

On one of those Mission nights in the Demesne, he recalled wistfully that he met a girl there. Hartnett had a romantic nature, though not every affair ended well:

I fell in love. I was sixteen at the time and had long passionate crushes but this was the real thing and it was heartbreaking because the girl became a nun. I wrote a lot of poems about this but only two were published as the rest were just effusions … I was able to write sonnets and strictly rhymed verse, containing all the bitterness that a sixteen year old can feel against the Church for stealing his girl. I maintained that God had a choice. He could have anybody He wanted but He chose this sixteen-year-old, snub-nosed, freckle-faced girl and He took her away from me. I was very bitter and I wrote a poem, entitled 'The Lord Taketh Away'.[14]

The poem was dedicated to Eileen Lohan:

> For her I wrote impotent songs
> transparent and slight as tears
> and offered her mortal happiness
> for some unspecified years
>
> But for her a death was
> the consequence of a kiss
> While Christ, as ghostly husband
> offered immortal bliss
>
> I fought, that devious lessons
> might somehow be undone,
> But the odds were three to one:
> Father and Son and Holy Ghost.
> I had no chance against such a Host.[15]

Yet Hartnett appreciated the ceremonial elements of Catholicism:

> It is easy to be sentimental about the past and to give one's childhood a cosmetic tint: but I do recall the tremendous awe at the grandeur of a High Mass, the darkened church in Holy Week, the excitement and magic of Midnight Mass – and I mean a religious magic, not a Santa Claus affair. These rituals were essentially tribal and made the community aware of its cohesiveness, aware of its Catholicism.[16]

However, his Mass-going memories were not always positive: 'When I was at school, Sunday was always a cold, wet morning, pale with the faces of reluctant, breakfast-less urchins herded together in a draughty church. Someone always fainted – me usually.'[17]

Looking back on it, Hartnett had an ambivalent attitude towards his upbringing in Newcastle West.

> There are as many things to love in a town as there are to hate. Indeed, the only things I disliked were class and priest-power, but if injustice is not seen to be done, such opinions are merely private prejudices. I remember, with pity for the man, a priest beating a child about a schoolroom for no good reason ... Newcastle West and its countryside provided me with images. Its neighbourhood is not spectacular: the mountains are miniature, the woods are copses at best. But it is soft, beautiful inland country, very green and over-lush in the summer.

As Paul Durcan put it, 'his childhood has been the mysterious well to which he has returned again and again'.[18]

Throughout the rest of his school years Hartnett continued writing. 'So the poetry went on, I had published another bad piece of verse in the *Irish Weekly Independent* and got a guinea for it. This brought me some small recognition in the town, as a few people there read the paper.'[19]

However, there was little hope of gainful employment in Newcastle West for a 'townie' like Hartnett. The major employers at the time were the County Council and two bottling plants, a few shopkeepers and, as Hartnett described it, 'the local hospital for the old and the unwanted'.[20]

'An air of hope and sadness always hung over the local railway station.' And it was from there that Hartnett, 'complete with cardboard suitcase and a single ticket to Euston', left home in 1961.[21] According to him, he went to London 'out of pure instinct'.

3

'The Emigrant Stint'

When Hartnett left Ireland in 1961, he 'went straight from Newcastle West for London, the furthest I had been since Lahinch, where I first saw the sea at sixteen. I saw Dublin vaguely, got on the boat and sailed away happily – to be greeted by the roar and smell of Euston'.[1] He was met by a friend, Jimmy Musgrave, who explained to him proudly 'the intricacies of the Underground, a tube full of evaporating people and old newspapers. I duly arrived in Kilburn. It looked pleasant enough on that summer's morning, with its neat houses and its rows of gelded elm-trees.'[2]

It being a Sunday, he went straight to bed. The next day he was introduced to the job his friend had lined up for him as:

> tea-boy in a factory that produced ovens and furnaces. It was my first glimpse of the worlds that men invent for themselves to make money – the hiss and the purple lightning of welders' torches, the aluminium dust from paint-sprayers and the runnels of liquid metal, red, white and searing.[3]

In this chemical gloom Hartnett made tea and warmed up meat pies four times a day. And every morning he swept a few acres of floor free of metal filings and fag ends. He did not stand it for long:

> Anyway I was getting tired, a feeling of hemmed-in exhaustion never

felt in the country. One day, having been paid, I emptied the contents of two packets of Epsom Salts into the tea-urn, served the tea, went out in the guise of going to the toilet and never came back.[4]

The money he'd made lasted a short while and once it was gone he went to work at a restaurant in Golders Green, as a table cleaner:

Then one day I realised that I had not written a line for months, an unusual thing for me at the time. For the first time I experienced the panic of young poets: I was wasting my life: death walked up and down the noisy kitchen. I was probably halfway through life and there was nothing done.[5]

He was just twenty years old.

The next day, he counted what money he had. It was enough to get to Dublin. There was a train leaving that would catch the mailboat at 8:45 that night. Hartnett went straight to Euston.

I walked around the damp, dirty station, thinking of the poor horde who would arrive in the morning, with their dark suits, white shirts, black ties and their brown cardboard suit-cases. I promised myself I'd never return to London, a promise I did not keep.[6]

His first time abroad was not an altogether positive experience. 'The English … having proved by various arguments that they were superior to Irishmen tried the "divide and conquer" approach with coloured people.' Hartnett disliked what he saw as the casual racism of the English. However, some of his other experiences abroad were happier. He encountered a kindred spirit:

who had also written poetry in Gaelic. [She]…was female, beautiful and a Gaelic poet from Connemara [Caitlín Maude]. I fell in love with her. We discussed poetry and the language over the next two-and-a-half years. I would have given a hundred English lyrics then if I had been able to write one Gaelic poem for her. My inability to praise her in the language she wrote so beautifully gave me a feeling of inadequacy ... I did not attempt to improve my pathetic knowledge at that time. [7]

In 1961, Hartnett collaborated with Maude on *An Lasair Choille [The Goldfinch]*, an Irish-language play that was first staged at An Taibhdhearc in Galway. The play was produced regularly throughout the 1960s, though not always to large audiences. Dominic O'Riordan of *The Irish Times* praised the 'haunting words' of *An Lasair Choille* at the Oireachtais Drama Festival where fourteen plays in Irish were staged at the Peacock Theatre in Dublin to very small crowds. The Peacock was 'as deserted as Goldsmith's village'. O'Riordan bemoaned this lack of popularity: 'A definition of a Dubliner is a man who does not go home for Christmas. A definition of a Gael is a man who does not attend plays in Irish.'[8]

This was a familiar complaint; that native Irish speakers were not necessarily interested in modern literature. As John Jordan put it:

I have an intuition (and some evidence) that many people perfectly fluent in Irish, don't give a drinker's curse for the best writing in Irish. This is not very peculiar. Possession of the Irish language does not bestow the Pentecostal gift of response to the artist's passionate vision of the ordinary or extraordinary.[9]

An Lasair Choille was the story of a young and rather naïve man exploited by a lame older man. He is made to work for his keep, persuaded by the older man that he would never survive in the outside world. The young man cannot choose between emigration to England, where he will have to work for a living, or staying in Ireland with a chance of inheriting wealth. The theme, that man is imprisoned by his weaknesses and fantasies just as the goldfinch is imprisoned by his cage, plays itself out. The goldfinch sings when let free. In the end the young man escapes. He survives.

Hartnett was not always gracious when accrediting Caitlín Maude for her input into their collaboration. In a letter to John Jordan he claimed that he was the main author. 'About the play: I was having a slight affair with a UCG student, Cáit Maude ... I wrote a one-act play ... she translated it ... (*An Lasair Choille*) a group of UCG students staged it ... I'm afraid she took the credit ...'[10] However, at other times, he was much more open about his relationship with her. It would appear to have been much more than 'a slight affair'. In another letter to Jordan, a year later, he was more forthcoming. The poem that he is referring to appears to be an early version of 'Short Mass':

25th Feb 1963

10 Leinster Avenue
North Strand.

... This poem is very important to me, not in the literary sense, but as a very telling part of my life ... I am continually being torn between my own atheism (if it is) and between women who are Catholic. I had the misfortune to have affairs with Catholic women only.

I couldn't clarify the poem for anyone but a few friends. The 'Catherine' in question is a real woman: you met her in McDaid's once. In the ceremonial mass what was once a brutal crucifixion is re-enacted as a painless joyful one … well my Catherine was attacked by a violent man a few years ago … not raped, but she was very shocked and after that, men were repulsive to her. She left the university and worked as a cashier in a Lyon's Tea-shop in London and then I met her and saved her … I was a child and she was a child … I saved myself too … That is my Mass: the sacrifice once more. I know I am only 21: it may be infantile. I would very much like to have it published. I have written a few short poems since and my language is developing though I am afraid all I may do is evolve a stylised method for recording impressions, like Hopkins.[11]

The poem was eventually published as 'Short Mass' many years later with the dedication 'For Caitlín Maude':

Listen,
If I came to you, out of the wind
With only my blown dream clothing me,
Would you give me shelter?
For I have nothing –
Or nothing the world wants,
I love you: that is all my fortune

But I know we cannot sail without nets:
I know you cannot be exposed
However soft the wind
Or however small the rain.[12]

Caitlín Maude (1941–1982) was an actress and a *sean-nós* singer, as well as a poet in the Irish language. She was very active on the poetry and music scenes in Dublin in the 1960s. Poetry readings and music were frequent events in some of the pubs around Grafton Street. Roy Lisker, the American writer and activist against the war in Vietnam, gave an outsider's account of one such occasion in 1969:

> It is easier to obtain general agreement about well-sung and well per-
> formed traditional Irish music than it is about contemporary verse.
> At every gathering there is at least one singer or instrumentalist, and
> they have a marvellous power to heal frayed tempers. Everyone will
> listen to Caitlín Maude singing folksongs in Irish … Music brings
> every session, no matter how stormy, to a mellow close.[13]

Hartnett and Maude had a tempestuous relationship. After their affair ended he wrote of a social encounter:

> Her diadem, pain, taut-lines on the skin-surface,
> and her eyes forever enfiguring tragedy …
> I knew she had her own life
> and we were both too dedicated to our arts
> to be dedicated to each other.
> I knew that her upheaval was violent
> when she chose corruption, chose to be vainglorious.
> but as I am cold, it took no violence in my soul
> to cease to sympathise.
> now when we meet (and we meet often,
> perhaps we do fear each other)
> we clash intellect with memory,
> and she never wins.
> but once she won, and left me mortal
> by a simple act: in company I met her
> after months: she was the honoured,
> her poetry had enthralled.
> she saw me and she
> (she and I who had laid naked body

to naked body, times before,
she and I who made a point
of being familiar with nipple, groin
and marking so we might never fully part)
she saw me and she
shook my hand.[14]

4

'YOU INSOLENT PUP'

Back in Ireland in autumn 1962, Hartnett was on the verge of being published as a result of a curious chain of events. Jimmy Musgrave from Newcastle West, who was over in London with Hartnett, was a nephew of the journalist Donal Foley. Foley read some of Hartnett's poetry, liked it and did a piece about Hartnett for the *Sunday Review* with the caption, 'Tea-boy of the Western World'. The article began, 'A big London engineering plant will shortly lose the services of its Irish tea-boy. He is going to America to devote himself to writing poetry.' It described Hartnett as 'the egghead tea-boy' who had been writing poetry since he was fourteen.[1] Asked what he thought of present-day Irish poets, Hartnett replied, 'I haven't read many of them, but those I have read are insipid.'[2] 'If he had been influenced at all by other poets, he could only think of three names – Gerald Manley Hopkins, T. S. Eliot and Yeats.'[3]

When Hartnett returned to Limerick he got a job as a postman. 'I had a fine job cycling around the countryside, finishing just after midday …'[4] As he told a reporter in later years, he didn't really care what job he did: 'I had absolutely no ambitions in any sphere except to write poetry.'[5]

Then came the next link in the chain.

I got a wild letter and numerous poems from Dublin from a young man called Paul Durcan early in 1962. He had read the article in the *Sunday Review*. He wanted my opinion of his work, and also to see some of my mine. His poems were mad, rich and full of classical allusions. I was delighted: there was another poet in Ireland. I sent him some of my poems.[6]

Paul Durcan called down to Newcastle West to meet him but Hartnett had gone to Galway to see a girl (probably Caitlín Maude).

I had missed meeting my first poet and was furious, but calmed down when my mother told me he had come in a car. So he was rich – and ordinary: from his poems I had expected him to come on a yak, at least.[7]

But Durcan had been busy. He had shown Hartnett's poems to a literary editor, John Jordan of University College Dublin (UCD):

Then, one morning in September, I was sorting the letters in the post-office and there was one for me with a Dublin postmark and in a strange hand. It praised my poetry, said six of my poems were accepted for *Poetry Ireland* and it also invited me to a reception to mark the launching of the magazine. It was signed John Jordan.[8]

Hartnett wrote back from Limerick giving some candid details of his life in County Limerick and also his views on his poetry. The haphazard punctuation is the writer's own, perhaps betraying his agitated state of mind at the time.

Dear Mr Jordan,

I was born here, Sept 18th 1941 … I became an atheist in '49 …

began to write (badly) in '55 … was violently in love in '58 … lost her (to God and convent) in '59 … lost interest in school … obtained a 'bad' Leaving Cert. in '61.

Father: alcoholic
Mother: rural, crude

… had play staged in Damer Hall (Irish play) in March … also in Ring, Waterford, and in the Galway Taibhdhearc … desire very much to attend UCD … but unfortunately, no money … to keep alive (and wanted) here, I decorate interiorially (badly) … have four brothers, one sister … I never take advice about my poems … I never revise … I haven't written for a year (degeneration owing to adverse conditions). I have to have learning around me – even a secondary school – to stimulate me. I speak like an incoherent Kerryman.

I may be going to Dublin on Thursday next … I never name any poems … considering it an unnecessary doing …

That's who I am,
Yours sincerely,
Michael Harnett[9]

Jordan then sent the proofs of the poems with suggested titles. Hartnett was slightly more serene in his next letter:

Dear Mr Jordan,

Thank you for remaking me. My feelings for my own work were near hate … but I re-read them all: there has been a reconciliation.

I have only known one person who was close to poetry … John Moriarty (UCD student) … but whatever he had was drowning under a net of classicism … I believed that a poem is born whole … that all revision is foreign … like putting an artificial limb on a child just born and already limbed … that to revise on the advice of a poet

40

is to bring the work close enough to his style to satisfy him ... on the advice of a critic is to accept the critic's opinion ... then what is produced is no longer a poem.

The proofs are fine, the titles are fine: but under no circumstances must 'Four Hounds' and 'Sulphur' appear in the same issue.

I shall send you most of the poems ... perhaps it's about time I got an opinion from someone in a position to give it.

All I wrote, I wrote while at school ... yet you know how far apart art and a secondary school are ... since I finished school, as a poet I am withering away ... I am only invulnerable in a cloak of learning ... I have to be with people who savour art ... however false their values ... I know quite a few UC students ... they are very stimulating ... I went to London last year ... I nearly went mad ... everything bad was very bad ... everything good was false. I'm nearly 21 ... when I am that ... I won't be allowed stay at home any longer (not that I want to stay).

And so back to hell,

Yours sincerely,

Michael Harnett[10]

Presumably Hartnett didn't want 'Four Hounds' and 'Sulphur' being published in the same issue, as they were similar in form and content, and appearing together would have reduced their impact.

In the end *Poetry Ireland* published just three of Hartnett's poems (still known as 'Harnett' as this stage) in the first instalment. Three other poems were kept back for future issues. It was, nevertheless, an astonishingly confident debut. Short, concise poems with vivid imagery were his speciality:

Sickroom

I know you cannot rise.

You are unable to move.
but I can see your fear,
for two wet mice
dart
cornered in the hollows
of your head.[11]

In 'Sulphur' the poet imagined himself as Zeus:

Sulphur
will engulf her
or else fire:
I am Zeus and I desire
her.[12]

On the day of the launch the intrepid young poet borrowed a suit, hitch-hiked to Dublin and set off to discover the literary world. Hartnett's introduction into this subculture was dramatic. Patrick Kavanagh had claimed that there was a standing army of Irish poets. Hartnett was now about to join its ranks and remembered the day vividly:

There is a myth current in Dublin, fostered by people who hope that if the number of poets writing is exaggerated, the quality of the poetry written is guaranteed to be mediocre, they preach the myth of the Thousand Poets, all equal, all equally minor. After a series of *Zhivago*-like coincidences I found myself being added to the Thousand on September 13th 1962.[13]

Poets in Dublin might not always have the best of reputations. 'The myth-makers say "spit into a Dublin pub and you'll spit on a poet" and they speak the truth – but only if they are aiming at a poet, and they usually are.'[14]

> I was very nervous on 13th September 1962. I had never met a poet before, let alone that revered and able personage, an editor. I found the Bailey and went in. I was too early, there were very few people there but a proliferation of liquor put me at my ease. John Jordan introduced himself and I found that he as an editor and as a man, lived up to my preconceived notions of reverence and ability.[15]

As the room filled up, Hartnett was shocked at the number of poets there were in Dublin, but a swift *per capita* comparison between Newcastle West and the capital showed him that the number was just. He discovered that 'poets and writers did not talk shop in pubs'. He heard snippets of gossip straight from the Vatican and the names of various racehorses. Soon a novelist was singing a bawdy song.

James Liddy was also present at the launch. He was hugely impressed by Hartnett. 'In the 1960s it happened again, a country-side opened to showcase a poet. Townlands spoke. Like Kavanagh, came out of the earth unstoppable.'[16] Liddy recalled the young poet's 'first caper' in literary Dublin: 'Ben Kiely in braces, Liam Miller leading the chorus, downstairs Richard Murphy in whisper-mutter with Ted Hughes and Sylvia Plath.'[17]

Once the reception in the Bailey was over, Hartnett was intro-duced to the delights of Dublin's premier literary pub, McDaid's on Harry Street. Again his hope for sparkling talk and literary conversation was to be disappointed. Instead, he heard, 'racing results, the rapid solution of world crises and the extra bonus of the shady love-lives of absentees'.[18] John Jordan introduced him to Patrick Kavanagh, McDaid's resident poet. Hartnett leaned over to shake his hand but Kavanagh declined, saying gruffly, 'I don't know him.'

Kavanagh had contributed a poem to the first edition of *Poetry Ireland*. Hartnett commented that the poem was not poetry at all, not realising that Kavanagh was still within earshot:

> I was young and foolish and not aware that Patrick Kavanagh was listening. He towered up, scattering drink on the floor, shouted 'you insolent pup' and left the table. I had not realised that he was the pub idol. I thought he was a boor. But he played to the stalls: he went into the pub for company and he had to make the best of the company he found.[19]

This encounter became notorious in Dublin's literary circle; the young prodigy confronting the old master. As poet and contemporary Michael Smith recalled:

> I recall him voicing his strong disapproval of Kavanagh's raucous behaviour in McDaid's, saying that if anyone in Newcastle West behaved like that, he would be barred from the pub, and why should a poet be made an exception of?[20]

Smith himself observed Kavanagh in McDaid's:

> Kavanagh could be, and often was ... indiscriminately abusive. But his critical standards were high and healthy; and an encounter with Kavanagh for the dilettante as often as not ended in a bloody execution.[21]

Yet Hartnett did make his peace with Kavanagh when he read his poetry later and as he put it 'saw that he was a poet indeed'. In fact, in the following years, Hartnett drank with Kavanagh and 'indeed backed horses with him'.[22] He dedicated 'The Poet Down' to Kavanagh:

> He sits between the doctor and the law
> Neither can help. Barbiturate in paw
> one, whiskey in paw two, a dying man:
> the poet down, and his fell caravan.
> They laugh and they mistake the lash that lurks
> in his tongue for the honey of his works.
> The poet is at bay, the hounds baying,
> dig his grave with careful kindness, saying:
> 'Another whiskey, and make it a large one!'[23]

For the next few years Hartnett 'sat in his company almost every day he was in town. After he died I heard actions and sayings attributed to him which he never said or did.'[24]

A *Sunday Independent* reporter had a few words with the young poet at the *Poetry Ireland* launch. He was full of plans for the future and said that he had completed a play which he had sent to the Abbey Theatre. It was called *A Swarm in August* and its theme was that of 'the Stage Irishman'. Not only that, he was not waiting on word back from the Abbey but had started work on another three-act play. 'Don't ask me how or why,' he said, 'it is an urge I have always felt. I just write and write.' He told the paper that he had written some 500 poems but had scrapped all but 150 of them.[25]

5

'I FAILED *CUM LAUDE*'

The first issue of *Poetry Ireland* contained a statement of intent written by its editor John Jordan:

> We are concerned with the publication of the best available verse by Irish poets or of special Irish interest, but we will attempt to include verse outside these categories, including translations. We are committed to no school, no fashion, no ideology. But we abhor mere opinion. We would wish in the humblest of ways to contribute to the re-creation of Dublin as a centre of letters. We hope we have the blinds up and the door on the latch.[1]

For Hartnett the door of opportunity was definitely on the latch. Not only did John Jordan publish him, he offered to sponsor his attendance at University College Dublin. As had been alluded to, in the correspondence between them, Hartnett could not afford to support himself at university.

At first Hartnett could barely believe his good fortune:

> Dear John,
> I can avail of your kind offer. I have found some of my own people in Dublin who will put me up free while I go to UCD.
>
> Doubting Thomas that I am please beg pardon: but please write and confirm your offer.
>
> You have made me extremely happy.[2]

Once he was convinced that the proposition was genuine, Hartnett wished to offer something in return if not to Jordan then to *Poetry Ireland*: 'Dear John, The next three poems and any more that are accepted I want to give free.'[3] It was little more than a gesture but Hartnett had his pride.

James Liddy also helped to encourage Hartnett to take up the deal. The 'always exuberant James Liddy', as John Montague put it, came from a more affluent background than Hartnett. The son of a doctor from Coolgreany, County Wexford, Liddy was a qualified lawyer and published poet. In a letter dated October 1962, Liddy kept Jordan up-to-date with developments, 'As regards Harnett, he is coming back in a short while with the paraphernalia of entrance. I got him the syllabus.'[4]

John Jordan had been a precocious talent, acting on the stage at the Gate Theatre with Micheál Mac Liammóir and Hilton Edwards when he was just fifteen, but he had decided to follow a literary rather than a theatrical vocation. The writer Leland Bardwell said Jordan:

> never wanted to leave the parties, and sometimes he'd sit up all night reading a detective novel. And if it was a Sunday morning, he'd wait till the various Masses were over so that his mother would assume that he'd been to church ... He was one of those thin angular men whom I thought resembled the caterpillar in *Alice in Wonderland*. He always sat sideways, frame bent, his long legs loped round each other. He had a long pulpy face with a lopsided smile.[5]

James Liddy also helped Hartnett out financially. According to Liddy, while Jordan 'gave him a pound a week for a year and talked of supporting him through First Arts in UCD, I contributed the day-to-day pint money of salvation ...'[6] Liddy was greatly impressed by the precocious young poet. He compared him to Patrick Kavanagh, which was high praise. There was an other-worldly attitude to Hartnett that Liddy discerned: with his 'bog fairy country accent, lilting, looking like a changeling'.[7]

Being published in the first two editions of *Poetry Ireland* established Hartnett as a serious poet, even at such a young age. As poet Macdara Woods put it: 'because it had breadth of vision and a consistently high standard of production, and always bore the hall-mark of its benign, and fastidious, editor, its influence – and his – has extended far beyond the final number in 1968'.

Liddy observed that 'Michael settled in through the poet-laden lanes of the never ghost-deserted city.' He began to acquire what he termed 'artistic temperament'.[8] Unlike many others, Hartnett was not intimidated by Patrick Kavanagh. On one occasion, as James Liddy recalled:

> Kavanagh swore by the magic of the opening of the Second Vatican Council but Michael said, 'I don't like the Pope.'
> 'Why not?'
> 'I don't like his clothes.'[9]

As Hartnett himself said in later years, 'arrogance is something you suffer from until you're eighteen, after that it's self-confidence'. And one could say that he certainly wasn't lacking in self-confidence.

Hartnett was very appreciative of the financial backing he was given.

> The fees which enabled me to spend my first year in Dublin in UCD were supplied by a man who suffers that rare disease in this practical world, generosity: a man who gave with no ulterior motive like

kindness, but merely because of the need of the recipient, and who asked for no interest, material or metaphysical.[10]

Hugh McFadden, a student in UCD at the time, remembered Jordan's influence: 'He was an outstanding, charismatic lecturer … who did with considerable charm what few other lecturers could do – both enlighten and entertain his students.'[11]

James Liddy, in a private letter in 1963 to Michael Smith, described him: 'John Jordan is a very complex, suffering being, strange, burnt-out when sober. He has lived his adolescence and young manhood as a flame and it takes a toll.'[12]

Michael Smith recalled Jordan as daunting:

Many students found him a rather forbidding figure, or at least, not someone to be approached casually or without considered purpose. And it is unquestionably true that he was a man who always appreci-ated the discipline of courteous formality, of taking the trouble to do things properly whether those things were literary or personal.[13]

And if he was severe as a teacher he could be even more so as an editor.

Mr Jordan was a more aloof – even awesome – editor for the young poet. Combining great intelligence and learning with a magisterial formality of speech and manner. In a society where poetry is generally associated with childhood or madness, one's meeting with Mr Jordan and coming to appreciate his dedicated involvement with poetry, gave it an importance that was vital encouragement for young poets to keep going.[14]

Thomas Kilroy echoed that sentiment: 'To us as students … he was remote and mysterious. The quick steps through the corridors of Earlsfort Terrace, that erect, upright carriage, that aquiline stare always directed over one's shoulder into the middle distance.'[15] Kilroy believed that it was necessary for Jordan to put on an air of inapproachability as he was little older than his students.

Liddy and Jordan had travelled down to Newcastle West to 28 Assumpta Park, the Hartnett family home. Liddy recalled that Hartnett's younger brothers were playing football outside: 'Denis the father already gone out and going out again. We went with him, we heard song and some fables of the West Limerick Labour Party.'[16]

Hartnett went to stay with the Liddys in Coolgreany on a number of occasions. Liddy's mother was unimpressed: 'Where does he come from? Newcastle West – a tinker's town.' But Hartnett was not discouraged. Liddy recalled him 'sitting on top of a pile of *Time* reading from a smaller pile. Michael could do this for days.'[17]

Hartnett studied logic and philosophy at UCD, although as he put it, his first and only year at university was not distinguished, which may have been an understatement. Michael Smith was a contemporary of his. Their attendance at university was sporadic, to say the least. To his knowledge, Hartnett 'almost never attended a lecture, so far as I recall. I was little better myself. The whole novelty of being university students was more than enough for us. Study was for others.'[18]

Even at this young age, Hartnett was supremely confident of his ability as a poet. 'I had never met any poet who was more assured of himself as a poet than Michael was. It was his destiny. All else seemed of secondary importance.'[19]

Liddy and Jordan sponsored Hartnett on the Dublin scene. As Liddy stated, 'Thereafter we ushered Michael into McDaid's

golden cave where he was given the treatment, coaxed, appraised'.[20]
Michael Smith recalled the appeal of McDaid's at the time.

> Kavanagh was holding his raucous court in McDaid's and there, too,
> could be found the Monaghan poet's new discoverers, John Jordan
> and James Liddy. Penniless young poets were treated to drinks by
> these two generous patrons ... and the place had a kind of attractive
> (at least to us) bohemian atmosphere in a squalid sort of way.[21]

As Smith put it:

> Writers need a place to meet and talk shop. In the old days of the
> Revival I suppose there were the few middle-class houses with their
> servants and well-disposed, if pretentious, hosts and hostesses.

However, poets now had to make do with pubs and, in his view:

> to most decent men, a pub is at all times preferable to a middle-class
> drawing-room; when the talk is boring there is always the drink (as
> much as he or his friends can afford), and when the company be-
> comes tiresome there is always the possibility of relief from a chance
> encounter ... I don't say that there are no disadvantages to a literary
> life having to survive in pub conditions: penury, alcoholicism [*sic*],
> parasitism, laryngitis are a few of the many hazards. Still, each and
> all seem preferable to a slow death by the stuffy lie ...[22]

In 1962, UCD was still in its city centre base, Earlsfort Terrace,
and had yet to move to its suburban campus of Belfield. Paul Durcan, Macdara Woods and Eamon Grennan also attended UCD at
the time. Grennan recalled:

student politicians like Gerry Collins and his cohorts stalking heron-eyed and three abreast down the long corridors … The smell of ink, sweat and books in the whispering library, murky productions of Beckett in the Little Theatre, readings of *Under Milk Wood* in Gaj's Restaurant.[23]

He also remembered 'an acerbic, probably hung-over John Jordan, mixing hate and love in equal measure for Spenser's *Faerie Queen* or turning to chastise a nun in the second row ("Please don't point that crucifix at me, Sister, I'm not the Devil, you know").'[24]

According to Macdara Woods, UCD at the time was a very conservative establishment:

If I seem to labour over-much a bleak university, undergraduate atmosphere in Earlsfort Terrace, it is because I sometimes find it hard to believe we could have been so constrained … We were students and I believe, repressed, any leaning towards love (as opposed to schmaltz) or poetry or joy was regarded as a dangerous adjunct to the grey-haired business of taking one's place. It was not possible then to point out that constraint and discipline are not at all the same thing.[25]

Eamon Grennan gives a detailed description of Hartnett at that time and remembered him as:

a small, compact figure in a dark, tweed jacket or overcoat, one hand in pocket, the other holding a cigarette. Large ears. A face of lovely planes, angles. The dark hair, combed forward to a little twist on his brow. Woodkern or novice monk, deep in English or Irish conversation, serious, watchful, intense, something dark and a bit secret there, no matter the smiles and talk over pints in Dwyer's or Hartigan's or McDaid's. Already a known poet.[26]

Leland Bardwell was living at this time at 33 Lower Leeson Street, which was conveniently close to the drinking establishments that the UCD students frequented. As a consequence, her home became a salon of sorts:

> They came from McDaid's, when the pub was closed; they came from the Bailey. John Jordan, still lecturing in UCD, arrived with a coterie of his own admirers, mostly students in their final year … The parties grew louder and louder. There was violence. Blood, booze and songs! And shiners! Very slippery, the outside world! … I use the epithet 'salon' with some irony … It makes me laugh to think of myself as a patron; the poor visitors never got a scrap to eat, and John Jordan – the only one of us with a steady income – paid for all the drink.[27]

Bardwell, rather unflatteringly described Hartnett as 'low-sized, wiry, like an anxiety-ridden monkey'.[28]

Having already been published, Hartnett was a minor celebrity among the literary circle at university. When Hugh McFadden first met the poet, in a pub on Leeson Street, he had already imagined Michael and tried to picture him from the voice of his poetry. 'He turned out to be somewhat different than I had imagined, not quite as tall, darker in hair colouring, more self-contained. But just as exotic, just as intense.'[29]

Hartnett had an encounter with one of his old heroes, Austin Clarke, although by this time Clarke was regarded by Hartnett and the other young poets 'as a remnant of the Celtic Twilight, honoured more for his years and his connection with Yeats and the Abbey than for his poetry ... Lorca, Eliot or Nietzsche were preferred ... Things Gaelic, things religious, things political were out.'[30] However, Hartnett was impressed by Clarke's technical ability, especially the way he used highly complex Gaelic metres in his poetry in English, and he remembered:

> In 1962 I was ... in digs in Leinster Avenue, North Strand. Walking from Leinster Avenue to the college, almost every day (no money) I sometimes saw a figure around the O'Connell Bridge area; broad-brimmed black hat, very white and plentiful hair and, unless memory is colluding with fantasy, a black cloak. 'Well,' I said to myself, 'he must be a poet, or some sort of artiste.'[31]

A journalist told him that the vision in black was, in fact, Austin Clarke. Hartnett had studied Clarke's poetic technique:

> I had become more fascinated than I ever had been with Austin Clarke's experiments in Gaelic metrics. Learning by rote and with much aborted attempts, I managed a ghostly notion of some eighty-four classical Gaelic metres – most of which had been handled with great skill and sometimes beautiful effect.[32]

He jumped at the chance to meet the old master:

> My landlady in Leinster Avenue considered Austin Clarke to be in league with the devil, because of his lifestyle and his attitude towards church and state. Sometime ... after a long party in Thomas Kinsella's house in Sandycove, I went into town for a cure. In McDaid's I met James Liddy and John Jordan. They were going to visit 'Mr Clarke' (as John Jordan always called him) in Templeogue. Would I like to come along? Oh, yes! A bottle of Advocaat was bought and we set

off. Only half-cured, I was looking forward to a glass of that soothing cream. The house was dim and full of books. Introductions were made and the bottle presented. The lady of the house disappeared into the kitchen; there was the reassuring clinking of glasses. The conversation was literary ... I contributed little to the conversation being overawed and my (then) usual silent self. In any case, I had one ear on the distant chinking. The lady of the house came out with a tray; on it, in all their glory were four mugs of tea ... I wept internally ...[33]

James Liddy's memory of the visit was somewhat different. The drink was different. 'The good sour poet, liked good sweet sherry ... we stopped before the door of an unornate man, we had in our charge a bottle of Bristol Cream.' The outcome was different as well. 'We waited while the bottle was taken. It stood awhile on a table, dreaming. Nora Clarke took it, brought it back with sandwiches.'[34]

However, Hartnett's time at UCD was not a happy period for him. The arrangement with Jordan was not without its drawbacks. While grateful for the support, Hartnett found the arrangement difficult as this letter from December 1962 demonstrated: 'Dublin, for many reasons, has brought me back to life. I am what I was, and better ... The receipts are here: perhaps it would be more convenient to pay by post (I hate this business tone)'.[35]

By February 1963, things had not improved:

I am in a very bad financial situation, father on the dole etc. I am going home on Tuesday to see if I can borrow £5 (for exam fee) from someone. If you have anything to spare I would be very grateful ... I hate begging ... but I have to ...[36]

Hartnett did not last long at UCD: 'My first and only year in university was not distinguished. I was more interested in the streets of Dublin …'[37] And when the exams came along he failed every subject. As he told Elgy Gillespie of *The Irish Times*, 'I failed *cum laude*',[38] simply because he didn't attend any lectures, but he had 'discussed philosophy at length in the pubs'.[39]

Not only was he unimpressed by academic learning, but Hartnett had found the financial arrangement with John Jordan problematical and was perhaps relieved that he could turn his back on it.

6

'TRUST NOTHING YOU WRITE'

Having dropped out of college, Hartnett, along with James Liddy and Liam O'Connor, edited *Arena*, a literary magazine; one of Dublin's many short-lived ventures. According to Hugh McFadden, '*Arena* complemented *Poetry Ireland* rather than competed with it.'[1] It published prose pieces as well as poetry (some early parts of James Plunkett's *Strumpet City* first saw the light of day in *Arena*) and was willing to publish non-Irish material. Liam O'Connor also wrote pieces on art and design.

It was an unusual situation in that Liddy was on the advisory board of *Poetry Ireland* along with James McAuley and Richard Weber. There was a certain level of competitiveness between Jordan and Liddy who were close friends. They had an intense friendship and periodic quarrels. Liddy seemed to enjoy the situation, on one occasion writing to Michael Smith with regard to *Arena*-related business on *Poetry Ireland* headed notepaper with the *Poetry Ireland* logo crossed out and the comment 'High Treason!' added in his own handwriting.[2]

The two publications perhaps reflected the personalities of their main movers. Jordan was a more austere figure than the high-spirited Liddy. Critical response to *Arena* was positive from the beginning. Desmond Fennell in the *The Irish Press* saw it as:

> the most exciting event in my fifteen years of conscious life as an
> Irishman ... *Arena* is unlike anything which has been offered to the

public for a long time … It is manna for the starved people. Having said that I have nothing else of importance to say except 'Read it'.[3]

Quidnunc of *The Irish Times* was also a fan: 'If you have half-a-crown to which you have no purpose assigned you might expend it on *Arena* … a very great deal of the magazine is taken up by miscellaneous writings, poems, essays and ejaculations from … James Liddy.'[4]

Aside from the fact that he was editing the magazine from his family home in Coolgreany, County Wexford (the headed notepaper for *Arena* had the phone number Inch 19), Liddy had the alarming habit of mislaying and sometimes actually losing writers' contributions. In praise of his contribution, Liam O'Connor wrote:

> *Arena* made considerable impact in its short life … an energetic, even vivacious platform for many of the young writers of the time as well as publishing the work of known and established writers. In this joint editorial activity Michael and I were helpers, but James was the editorial spring. It was his genius which lifted the magazine and gave it its buoyancy of spirit.[5]

It is doubtful whether *Arena* provided a regular income for Hartnett. However, it did pay well for its time. As Thomas McGonigle recalled jocosely: 'James Liddy … ruined my life. In the spring of 1965 … he paid me four guineas for what became my first published poem.' This was quite a substantial payment for any poet in the 1960s, let alone a beginner. McGonigle was only slightly put out that he had had 'to spend one of those guineas on a round of drink in O'Dwyer's on Leeson Street'.[6]

McGonigle may have been paid four guineas but Patrick

Kavanagh received £20 for one poem.[7] Negotiating with the likes of Patrick Kavanagh could be difficult. According to Liddy, dealing with the elderly poet always involved 'rough bargaining'. While negotiating permission to use 'A Summer Morning Walk', he recalled, 'I was late that day opening the tower, delayed by the hardy business of poem-buying from Kavanagh in McDaid's ... We had concluded with "luck money" and a handshake.'[8]

Kavanagh was given £20 for the poem, owing to its length. However, before publication, he edited it down into a much shorter version, but did not offer to refund any of the £20. Liddy's relationship with Kavanagh could be volatile as they met most days in McDaid's. As Liddy recounted, 'The language of the premises was Irish-rural':

'It's five pounds to talk to me today.'
    'Paddy, it's usually only a pound, even on a bad day.'
    'But it's a black day for me – hand over or fuck off.'
    Liddy held up a one-pound note.
    Paddy took it and savagely, if calmly, tore it to little pieces ... Some gent got down on his knees, and in that small lounge behind the single pillar, scooped the green remnants up. It now hangs, framed and described, on a suburban wall.[9]

Arena was hardly a good business proposition; it was subsidised in the main by Liddy's mother, 'my dear mother, a one-woman Arts Council' as he himself deemed her.[10] *Arena* had a certain boisterous, irreverent attitude, perhaps a reflection of Liddy's extrovert nature. The early issues had contained serious notes on the contributors but, by the end, they were filled with cod biographies. In a typical example, James Liddy was portrayed as someone who was 'distributed among two professions, three houses, and a thousand friends, he will not last the pace'. According to *Arena*, Patrick Kavanagh was 'a bard, whom it is dangerous to revere', and Michael Hartnett was described as 'Born County Limerick, favourite film star – Sophia Loren'.

Arena did, on occasion, take itself seriously:

> Note to the young poets. Allusions of any kind are fatal because they have been done before and have become a style. Use of another poet's method is influence. Wait. A year, or two or three mean nothing when you are under thirty. Your real enemy now is enthusiasm. Trust nothing you write.[11]

Poetry Ireland received some support from the Arts Council. *Arena* did not. In essence, the Council guaranteed *Poetry Ireland* up to a maximum of £50 against any losses per issue. The first issue made a loss of £93 6s 9d. Jordan was frequently disheartened. 'The Irish do not buy literary magazines if they can possibly beg them, borrow them, steal them or riffle them in bookshops. When it is a question of a magazine devoted solely to verse the situation is aggravated.'[12] Jordan suggested that poetry had more writers in Ireland than readers:

> All Irish adults and many Irish children write verse but in most cases they prefer reading their own verse to anybody else's … In Dublin you can throw a stone into almost any licensed premises and you're bound to hit a poet. The place is alive with them. Yet a poetry magazine can well die with them.[13]

Michael Longley, who attended Trinity College at the time, was impressed by the new magazine. 'We did get a whiff of UCD at its best when in 1962 John Jordan revived *Poetry Ireland* … it was then a rigorously skinny magazine and acceptance mattered a lot … Jordan took our apprentice pieces seriously.'[14] Macdara Woods was of a similar view:

> It is in the nature of small poetry magazines to be courageous, news-sheets from the barricades, and this new *Poetry Ireland* was certainly courageous, but it also had intelligence and grace. Austere is a word which has often been used of John, and to some extent I suspect this is another way of saying he was never vulgar.[15]

Jordan himself wrote of the pressure he felt under as an editor of a magazine that was one of the few outlets for new voices in poetry:

> Of those versifiers, every second one is convinced that he or she is the object of deliberate malice on the part of poetry editors. No wonder, what with beggars, borrowers, thieves, rifflers, poetasters and the un-justly done-to, that the existence of an Irish poetry magazine is, at best, precarious.[16]

Hartnett was certainly not living a comfortable life at the time. Liddy recalled his surprise at Hartnett's appetite on one occasion. 'I remember his hunger, how he ate all the butter on the table in the Glenworth Hotel.'[17]

In the summer 1963 edition of *Arena*, Hartnett's translation of the *Tao* was included as an inset on the centre pages. He dedicated the poem:

> For my three friends
> My father who is a Taoist
> James Liddy who tries to be a Taoist
> And John Jordan who should be a Taoist.[18]

In an interview with Dennis O'Driscoll, Hartnett claimed that his father had been a 'socialist with Taoist leanings, though to say this is to talk with hindsight'. Hartnett added mischievously, 'Like all poets I can foretell the past.'[19] Hartnett told O'Driscoll that, during his time in England, he had developed his interest in Chinese beliefs: 'In London in 1960, I did judo and was interested in the philosophy, especially Taoism. It contains very much an Irish sensibility: things happen, you direct your fate (though I'm not a fatalist or anything).'[20]

However, the poet told Hugh McFadden that he had started work on an early version of the *Tao* when he was only seventeen, and had completed it while working as the caretaker of the James Joyce Museum in Sandycove.[21] Dolly Robinson, widow of Lennox Robinson, had been the first caretaker. According to Robert Nicholson, she was reputedly 'fond of a drop' and did not last long.[22] James Liddy had been the second curator of the tower, Hartnett the third. Liddy claimed that he got Hartnett the job: 'Michael used to invite his girl-friend to a sleeping bag on the floor of the museum, in the morning they would wash in the pools among the rocks, Dedalus and nymph.'[23] Rory Brennan recalled encountering him there:

> I first met him when he was curator, or doorkeeper as he might have put it, of the newly opened Joyce Tower ... He was reading a William Faulkner novel. He indicated the book, pronouncing 'I prefer him', and then waved dismissively at the Joycean memorabilia, waistcoats and all.[24]

Paul Durcan, in his poem 'Ulysses', described an episode at the tower when his father John Durcan, a district court judge, attempted to get his hands on a copy of James Joyce's book:

'Mr Hartnett, I understand you stock copies of a book entitled *Ulysses*, I would like to purchase one copy of same.'

'Certainly, Your Lordship, certainly,' replied the ever-courteous curator. Formally he handed it over, as if delivering to some abstract and intractable potentate a peace gift of a pair of old shoes.

'Thank you, Mr Hartnett.'

The curator, at his most extravagantly unctuous, replied: 'Very glad to be able to oblige you, Your Lordship.'[25]

The job did not appeal to Hartnett. His favourite item in the tower was the key. 'The key to the door was huge and was always a great conversation piece when he took it out of his pocket.'[26] His time at the tower was not entirely unproductive; it influenced the translation of the *Tao* which he had been working on for some time. In fact, Hartnett's version of the *Tao* was a very free adaptation as he readily admitted:

This is not a translation. I know no Chinese. In 1963 I was curator of Joyce's Tower in Sandycove. I read a Victorian translation of the *Tao Te Ching* and could see the beauty of the philosophy beneath the translator's ugly prose. I did this version to satisfy myself. The imagery is a mixture of Oriental, Occidental and mystical. The landscape is that of Sandycove, the tower and the sea. I hope that after all this tampering, the philosophy at least is intact.[27]

As he told Dennis O'Driscoll some years later:

I didn't know any Chinese at the time but went out of the way to pick up a few characters, or rather to learn a few characters. Actually, I picked up a few characters as well in Chinese restaurants; but that's another story![28]

In its short life *Arena* showed a dynamism and lightness of spirit. As one outside critic put it:

> *Arena* lived without regard for exactness of fact and typography, which angered people for whom a magazine is judged only by its regularity and correctness in both. However *Arena* lived with flair. Its editors and contributors cavorted, were reputed to run the periodical from McDaid's, refused to take life seriously. Much of this was true.[29]

The final editorial in *Arena* concluded, 'The door of the nearest pub stayed open all day and we drank like prodigal sons. Now we think Spain would be a cheaper drinking life.'[30]

Hartnett went to Spain a number of times, specifically to learn Spanish so he could translate Lorca.[31] His left-wing views did not prevent him from enjoying the life in Spain, then in the last few years of General Franco's long regime. As he put it:

> he is dying, the coin adorner
> and he will be mourned
> for what are principles in face
> of cheap wine, cheap cigarettes?[32]

James Liddy accompanied him on one occasion. It was to Spain that 'two-thirds of the Editors took themselves after the last double issue, to wind down its legacy in piles, dalliance and punning'.[33] Liddy's account of the trip shows that it was not just a literary expedition:

> The 't' had not yet come into 'Harnett', there was still a not quite defined volatility, the countryman was there but the countryman

in the city had not consolidated … Michael, Barry Cusack and I arrived in Malaga airport and shortly afterwards found ourselves in a basement bodega with young white-aproned guardians of the wine. Each order was on the slate, and at the end of a stretched evening we offered to pay but no one knew the amount.[34]

Hartnett later wrote about that night and an argument that erupted with Liddy:

We have sat in Malaga
arguing over servant's ways
We have sat in Malaga
mistaking love of the master
for love of what the master pays.[35]

Liddy was unbothered by Hartnett's socialist leanings:

We came to a late sore point, part of the class malaise of that time. I was talking about my capricious adorable mother and her temperamental, wonderful housekeeper Josie Reynolds who was her friend. Michael would have none of it, there was no equal ground between housekeepers and mistresses, the former work and live in because they are paid … He insisted Josie stayed with us as she thought there was no alternative in her desperate life.

By the end of the night they couldn't recall how much they had drunk:

Further crisis engulfed us, according to custom the rounds were not paid for but left to the end – the *casa* had been lively, the waiters nipping, no one bothered to record anything. We came to a hand-shaking arrangement and walked up to the fresh air, let it clear the world of a reign of fog.[36]

The trio's intentions may have been literary but they enjoyed themselves too.

Next morning a tram to the beach but we had no time to contemplate a swim: a row of bar-restaurants knelt invitingly on the sand with fresh fish cooking … Talking is a reflection of landscape and we were instantly lyrical …

I got a swim on the beach next to the rock of Gibraltar, Michael guarding the heap of my possessions, we leant away from the monkeys and did not cross over into that portion of empire.[37]

However, the trio did make their way to Morocco, which had its own attractions: 'Michael must have got some *keif* somewhere; our bus was stopped by the police, and Michael in his agitation let some fall. It spilled across the floor but the officials were not interested in tourists.'[38] In Hartnett's own version of the incident:

he saw the police approaching and at a moment when they weren't looking in his direction he put his hand, full of *keif*, out of the window and let the wind blow it away. He placed the pipe on the floor and owing to the bus having stopped on an incline it rolled away from him down the bus.[39]

The trio soaked up the local culture. Liddy enjoyed the atmosphere. 'We went to a club and young Arab girls danced, at least Barry and Michael thought they were girls.'[40]

However, having returned to Dublin by the end of 1964, the young poet felt isolated. By the mid-1960s, the scene in Dublin was losing much of its impetus. James Liddy had left for San Francisco to take up a teaching post. Even John Jordan had left. According to Hugh McFadden:

… his life in Dublin seemed to have closed in on him; the strain of lecturing. Writing and reviewing and much 'socialising' with his friends in McDaid's had begun to take its toll. He took a leave of absence from his staff post in UCD.

Jordan took up a position in Newfoundland.

The farewell party for him in the Bailey was memorable; it being the time of flower power, the poet Paul Durcan purchased red roses from a stall at the corner of Grafton Street and bedecked the tables and those sitting at them with these regal flowers.[41]

According to Durcan, Hartnett had a disdainful attitude to alcohol at the time:

In the early 1960s Michael Hartnett spent a great deal of time in the pubs but he was different from all the other drinkers in that he was contemptuous of the culture of alcohol that ruled at that time, especially in the literary pubs.[42]

Durcan recalled being shocked by the 'severity of his strictures'. There were three types of drinkers which he condemned:

the elderly writer publicly in the grip of alcohol addiction … No poet should allow himself to become vulnerable to such an extent … Bohemian drinkers who regarded it as obligatory to offer up one's life on the altar of alcohol, and who preached a cult of alcohol … the lawyer-journalist-academic types who were so besotted with alcohol that no matter how witty their conversations and writings, their thinking was sodden with booze.[43]

His stern attitude may have been influenced by his perception of his father's heavy drinking. Observing Patrick Kavanagh in his last alcoholic years may have also shaped his views. Durcan was surprised at this stance in the 1960s. Amid a culture permissive of heavy drinking Hartnett was willing 'to be a heretic and to stand outside everybody'. He admired Hartnett's independence of mind and the courage it required. 'His ruthless common sense could be mistaken for arrogance and his high standards for conceit.'[44]

Hartnett felt that his position at *Arena* had closed some literary doors to him in Dublin, so he decided to emigrate and, on 13 January 1965, he was on the Irish Sea again, London-bound.[45] He had 17s 6d in his pocket.[46]

7

'Golgotha, Gentlemen, please'

For the next few years Hartnett lived mainly in London, though he spent some time in Spain and Morocco. While he was away in Morocco his grandmother Brigid Halpin died at the age of eighty-three. He was unable to make the funeral and he felt guilty about that for the rest of his life. As he put it in 'Death of an Irishwoman': 'I loved her from the day she died'. He described that poem as his 'apology' to her.[1]

Emigration was the fate of most of his school class. In an article for *The Irish Times* written in 1969, Hartnett examined the fate of his Newcastle West primary school sixth class of 1955. Of the class of thirty-nine, thirteen were in England, eight were in Dublin and only seven were still in Newcastle West. As he put it, Newcastle West is:

a town that is not dying. It has kept its economic stability at a terrible price, the constant exportation of human beings. It is an example of a town that is alive because the young leave, a town that would certainly be ruined if these people born in the 1930s and 1940s had stayed at home en masse. The enemy is not England, not Dublin, it is in the town itself. It fails to attract and it fails to employ.

Hartnett recalled one young man who had left the town because of its social snobbery. The reading of those peoples' names who had paid their dues, 'omitting those who had not or could not, markedly, because the names were read in street order so everyone knew who had reneged. The decency of the good, he said was turned to pride and the poor were stigmatised.'[2]

> Why did the better dressed and richer people sit to the front and middle of the church on Sunday and the poor sit right and left, or stand in the porch? Why were the poor branded and why could the poor not face their God on Sunday? Were they less religious than the rich?[3]

The young man told Hartnett that he had lost his religion 'because he could not walk to the altar rails with a hole in his trousers, or kneel to God because of a tattered shoe: "God may have been at my face but the sneering population were behind me".' When Hartnett suggested to the man that he was too proud and that a Christian should be humble, he replied, 'Humility should not be enforced.'

Hartnett met many of his fellow emigrants from Newcastle West while in England. 'If I had a job tomorrow, I'd go home,' they told him. But returning emigrants did not have it easy either:

> But they know there is a problem of integration, they have encountered it when they come home on holidays. It is mainly of their own making. They usually mock the ways, the wages, the deadness of the place and what is worse they manage to acquire an obnoxious London slang which they imagine to be a better English than that spoken in Newcastle West. The people at home resent this, rightly.[4]

And to make matters worse 'if the emigrants do come back to stay the many snide remarks that hint at failure make life unpleasant'.

He was amused that in Newcastle West there was a differ-ence in status based on the destination of the migration. It was believed in the town that 'to go to England' suggested poverty but 'to go to Dublin' suggested cleverness at school. Hartnett was also critical of the racial attitudes of some of his fellow countrymen in London. While the English looked down on the Irish, the Irish in turn looked down on others:

> My money lasted a short while and I became involved in Irish ghetto life. A minority, degraded everyday by their 'fellow' workers, consid-ered to be on the same level as 'blacks' (which comparison they tried to disprove by hating the coloured races fiercely), what can they do, but occupy the same houses, frequent the same pubs, dance in 'Irish' dancehalls and constantly try to prove their equality by drinking and fighting? They did not mind being called the 'drunken' or 'fighting' Irish: give an Irishman a nickname and he gets the feeling of being wanted. They just used the only means in their power to become an accepted part of lower-class London.[5]

However, it was not all hardship for Hartnett. It was while in London that he met his wife to be, Rosemary Grantley. Accord-ing to *The Holy Door* literary magazine of 1965, 'Hartnett recently announced his engagement to Rosemary Grantley. At present, in hospital with complications following appendicitis where he is writing a science-fiction novel.'[6]

Rosemary recalled:

> Michael and I were introduced by mutual friends on 16 May 1965. It was love at first meeting. We all went drinking that night and Michael dominated the proceedings with his constant flow of jokes and witticisms and sparkling conversation. Subsequently he arrived

for our first date with his emigrant's suitcase full of the collected, and mostly unpublished, works of Michael Hartnett to date. At the end of the evening I was convinced I was in the company of someone very special. He had an astounding amount of knowledge on a huge variety of subjects and what he didn't know he made up (although of course I did not know that at the time!). He also had a lovely tenor voice and would sing arias from the opera to me – notably the 'Flower Song' from *Carmen*. I was getting the full treatment! On our second date he brought with him a love poem he had written for me. I was completely bowled over and from that time on we were inseparable day and night. We didn't go out much in the early days but spent much time recounting our personal histories, opinions and ambitions. Although unpublished in book form at the time, Michael had supreme self-confidence in his poetic abilities ...[7]

Rosemary Grantley was well travelled, having lived in America for a year. She had also taught English in Spain and resided in Switzerland for a time. Many of the poems that Hartnett composed at the time were inspired by his new love:

> I will pay court to you
> after an antique Irish fashion
> and if you delight in singing
> I will sing[8]

Even while in his sick bed Hartnett was full of projects and, irrespective of his 'science-fiction novel', he did have ambitions to write fiction at this time: 'Michael wrote this period up in an unpublished novel.'[9] Hartnett had planned to write novels before and had had an extract from a short novel – a prose piece entitled 'Golgotha, Gentlemen, Please' – published in *Arena* in the summer of 1964. In 1966 *The Holy Door* also included a different extract from the same work. These excerpts were the only parts of 'Golgotha' that surfaced in public. The *Arena* extract described an urban nightmare. *The Holy Door* chapter almost seemed from a different work altogether, such was its difference in form and in tone; it had a rural setting and strong autobiographical elements. There appeared to be little connection between the two parts and the novel was never published. In 1978, Brian Lynch, then involved with the Writers Co-op, wrote to Hartnett asking if he 'thought it was worth digging up again', with a view to publication.[10] Nothing came of it.

Hartnett's notebook from this period in London contains a plan for a novel, including a rough map of the town in which it was set, with just a couple of scenes actually written. From the notes it appears to have been a novel about rural repression and small-town bigotry, a familiar enough theme for Irish fiction at the time, distinguished only by its experimental organisation, a dual narration, with the male and female protagonist each narrating their versions of the same scenes.[11] Again, nothing came of it, though the basic plot and theme was very similar to that of the poem 'The Retreat of Ita Cagney'.

Hartnett and Grantley visited Ireland to meet Hartnett's family and stayed for a while at Corrigmore, James Liddy's family's summer residence in Kilkee, County Clare. Liddy had, in his own words, turned the house there 'into a bardic refuge centre'. He recalled how 'Rosemary, Michael's fiancée, arrived for a rest before presentation to her future in-laws across the Shannon ...'

One of the regular disputes between Hartnett and Liddy erupted:

> An intermittent huge dispute paced itself ... Michael on the technical side, for knowledge and practice of prosody, alliteration, for reflecting

rhyme schemes in English and Irish, me for Pound's and Olson's breath, for *vers libre* for Beat extravaganza and open form …[12]

The verse Hartnett composed, describing the incident displayed his optimism at the time, and his admiration for Liddy:

We have argued over style
in the grey sheltered limestone bays
of Clare and not agreed: but we
shall be poets in coming days[13]

James Liddy wrote a slightly fictionalised version of Rosemary's meeting with Hartnett's family. Paul Durcan was also with them. (In it Liddy called Rosemary 'Denise Marie', but left Michael (Mike) and Paul with their real names.) Liddy drove them from Kilkee where they had been staying, but before they left Hartnett borrowed £16 from Liddy so he could afford to buy Rosemary a present and still have enough money to get them back to London.

Being English, Rosemary was apprehensive about how she might be received. In the car she seemed edgy. From the driver's seat, Liddy observed them in the mirror:

'Why do you have your hair like that, Paul, all over the place?'
'That's the way it grows.'
'Would you like to comb it and let it settle down?'
'Be as it may.'
'It would look much nicer.'
'I haven't got a comb.'
'Mike, will you lend Paul your comb?'

Paul slid it through his matted mop and handed it back gingerly, muttering how his great-uncle (Major John MacBride) had been shot by the English but refused to be blindfolded, saying he had never been afraid to look down the barrel of an English gun. Michael whispered to Rosemary not to push it any further.

They stopped in a couple of pubs along the way. Rosemary was anxious for them to keep moving. The men drank stout. Rosemary drank tomato juice. Eventually they got to West Limerick.

> Mike's father had the same face and the same pair of glasses as James Joyce, and, if his son was to be believed, the same capacity for the stuff. The mother made tea and put up a ham salad almost as soon as we were in the kitchen.[14]

The father liked Rosemary: 'I didn't know they made them that good across the water.'

After they were shown the family photo album they headed for what everyone called the 'Blueshirt' pub – a ramshackle place with a stove in the middle and a picture of Michael Collins on the wall, but as the father remarked, 'it serves pints'.

The men talked politics. Denis Harnett held forth. 'Mind you now, I was against them. My father threw me out of the house there in Maiden Lane for going against the Griffiths/Collins crowd. We thought they were the shopkeepers, the big farmers' men …'

The ladies were on one side of the table with port, gin and orange, their eyes glazed over with such talk. In a corner, Paul Durcan languished with toothache. Treaty politics made no difference to him. Rosemary concentrated her gaze on Mike. His eyes signalled back, 'Don't worry, they like you, they're too shy to say so.'

The father told them how he broke with Fianna Fáil:

It was Emergency Order No. 93 of 1941, I was working on the bog then and remember it well. It lowered the hourly minimum wage to nine pence, and what with the missus and Mike just happening then, it was a hard day's work and no porter after it …

The real subject of the evening was Rosemary, but she was not mentioned, being exotic and as far away from them as the moon.

As always it was a tough one for the English but Rosemary broke from under her stiff upper lip. She got up from the women's side of the table and tripped to where Mike sat half-asleep. While everyone looked at her she planted herself on his knee, putting up her smooth face and kissing him, defying the entrenched atmosphere of eloquence and aridity.[15]

Rosemary Hartnett remembered the occasion differently:

I have never drunk tomato juice but was met with a blank look in the local pub in Newcastle West when I first asked for a Martini and then a Dubonnet … I wouldn't dream of making such personal remarks to Paul Durcan or even to my best friend! In truth I was a little in awe of this strange, wild young poet.

According to Rosemary, the men teased her unmercifully about the way the English had subjugated the Irish:

They drove me all over the countryside pointing out the Big Houses where the landlords had ruthlessly oppressed the peasants, starving them and harnessing them to their coaches. They ensured that I returned to England with a gigantic guilt complex.[16]

8

'THE ZEAL FOR METRE AND SYLLABLE'

Hartnett and Rosemary Grantley married in 1966, in England. In 1968, they had a daughter and called her Lara, after the poems by Pasternak which Hartnett had first come across in Newcastle West Public Library when he was seventeen. In August 1968, Hartnett told *The Irish Times*, 'I am coming back to Dublin in the middle of August, whether I have a job or not'; an announcement, according to the paper, that was said 'with Joycean arrogance, but reversing the Joycean direction'.[1] Hartnett added that he was working on a film script based on the story of *Diarmuid and Gráinne*. He told a journalist that he had returned to Ireland with the same amount of money in his pocket as he had left with three years earlier: seventeen shillings and sixpence.[2] His wife remembered it differently:

> My father lived in Australia and we had applied to Australia House to emigrate there, sponsored by him. Then Michael asked me that since I didn't want to remain in London would I consider going to live in Ireland. I acquiesced and our fate was sealed! We had a couple of hundred pounds saved for this – not 17/6d! Michael preceded me but by the time I joined him six weeks later, all the money was gone and we lived hand to mouth for several months …[3]

He knew that he could not make a living from poetry alone, so alternative means of income had to be found. His employment record was erratic, to say the least. He had his own explanation of his restlessness: 'To hold twelve jobs in eight years may point to basic instability, shiftlessness, or plain laziness but it really betrays the panic that descends on a person with a confirmed literary bent.'[4] Tea-boy, dishwasher, postman, chef, house painter, security guard and caretaker of the Joyce Museum were among the occupations he had tried.

Hartnett got a job as a night telephonist at the telephone exchange on Exchequer Street. Publisher and poet Michael Smith was a drinking buddy at the time. According to him, Hartnett found the job 'boring and was only too glad to escape from it (even during working hours) and head for O'Neill's of Suffolk Street to drink pints with some other of his escapee colleagues from the exchange'.[5]

It was a common complaint of writers at the time, and still is to this day. As Michael Smith stated, 'Poetry doesn't pay. Most young poets know this. They know too, that poetry is not written to pay, and therefore they do not grumble that it doesn't'.[6] They may have known it, but it didn't stop them grumbling. The optimism of the early 1960s had disappeared.

With the collapse of magazines such as *Poetry Ireland* and *Arena* there were few available outlets, and even less available income, for young writers. In April 1969, Quidnunc of *The Irish Times* criticised the writer Hayden Murphy who, on the *Sunday Miscellany* radio programme – rarely a source of controversy – had spoken of his inability to make a living from his poetry. In Quidnunc's opinion, it was:

what can only be described as a bleat … repeating a moan that has been typical of such people for a tiresomely long time. Why, he wanted to know, were poets so undervalued and underpaid? Why had a poet whom he specified by name [Hartnett] to eke out a living as a night telephone operator? Why – the gist of his argument seemed to be – were not poets subsidised by the State, set up in sound-proof, ermine ivory towers, and kept in comfort while they framed their immortal lines?

The trouble with a statement like this is that the listener has no immediate chance to answer. On Sunday, for instance, I had no chance to say that if a man has poetry in him – or any real creative gold – it will come out whether he's a binman or a brewer. I had no chance to point out that, in the absence of night telephone work in his day Billy Shakespeare ostled horses before he reached the eminence where Burbage would throw him a tired plot and say; 'Ere Will, write us a workin' tragedy on that, will ya?'

I had no chance to say that Piers Plowman worked at his trade, or to mention that, of contemporary Irish poets, Kinsella is a civil servant, Padraig Fallon was an Excise man (like Burns), Patrick McDonogh was a very efficient executive with Guinness, Donagh MacDonagh was a lawyer, while his father, another poet, was a teacher, and Francis Ledwidge was a road-worker … Nor had I any chance to say to the moaning young man on the radio that what Yeats probably meant was: 'Irish poets, learn a trade.' And then, if a great gold of poetry is there, it will be mined anyway.[7]

Unsurprisingly, some of the targets took umbrage. They composed a joint letter to *The Irish Times*:

The tendency of Quidnunc's remarks of payment for poetry is to suggest that poets ought to be content with the present wretched standard of payment, and with the lack of encouragement for poetry in Ireland now, and to support themselves by honest trades like road-mending.

The broadcast Quidnunc objected to was made by Hayden Murphy who once worked a milk-round from 3 a.m. to 10 a.m. every morning and is at present obliged to be away in England by the financial problems of producing his magazine *Broadsheet*. We wish to repeat his main statement, that writing poetry is work: that nothing is being done in Ireland to make it easier for a poet to live by his work (as opposed to commemorating dead poets) and that far from demanding to be isolated in ivory young Irish poets are asking for the opportunity to take their work into public and be fairly paid for it.[8]

The letter was signed by Leland Bardwell, Eiléan Ní Chuilleanáin, Michael Hartnett, Pearse Hutchinson, Caitlín Maude, Macdara Woods and John Jordan, among others.

It was a familiar theme. Michael Smith and Trevor Joyce in their magazine, *The Lace Curtain*, argued that:

Dublin as a literary centre is a myth, the work of Bord Fáilte ad-men, an indigenous multitude of tenth-rate non-poets and bombastic shamrock-nationalists (mostly, thank God, in exile). Mr Haughey's tax-concessions are irrelevant to the Irish artist who must either work full-time at some mundane job or else never earn enough to be taxed anyway.[9]

Hayden Murphy himself described his life at the time:

Two years have gone by since I decided to attempt making my living by writing. It has been a strange two years; often desperate, even despairing. The early cold of a milk round, combined with an attempted routine day of writing, is not really effective.[10]

However, he was still optimistic:

A break appears to be appearing: the young writer of the 1960s is prepared and able for the 1970s. Writing, a craft known for the numbers it attracts, the flattering way it allows you dabble with the idea of genius and that discerningly callous way it can reject you, seems at last to be taking care of its children.[11]

Hartnett was one of those young writers, but now he had a family to support – after Lara in 1968, a second child, Niall, followed in 1971 – and he took a more cautious attitude to employment. He maintained his job as telephonist and supplemented his income by reviewing. The young family had moved to St Aidan's Park, Marino, and later relocated to Foxfield Road, Raheny. Rosemary Hartnett traced her husband's heavy drinking to this period:

We were mightily relieved to be saved from the edge of starvation by Michael securing a job as night telephonist but the elation didn't last and Michael gradually came to hate the job … He took as much official and unofficial time off as possible and his pay cheques (already meagre) would suffer as a result.[12]

The Dolmen Press published Hartnett's first collection, *Anatomy of a Cliché*, in May 1968: a set of love poems dedicated to his wife: 'To Rosemary, in an effort to convey some of the overtones neglected by the conventional phrase, I write you these poems'.

It received less than unanimous praise. The cliché referred to in the title was 'I love you': the first seven poems in the sequence were entitled 'Mo Ghrá Thú', 'Te quiero', 'Je t'aime', 'Ich liebe dich', etc. Douglas Sealy in *The Irish Times* was not overly impressed:

Mr Hartnett's *Anatomy* does not attempt to dissect and lay bare the workings of that odd mixture of carnality and spirituality known as love but it is an effort to convey some of the overtones neglected by the conventional phrase … Mr Hartnett's poems, which give the impression of being formed with a certain careless rapture in the white heat of inspiration, do not as might have been expected, despise the use of conventional imagery … Mr Hartnett might have written better in an earlier age, or if he found a style to curb his waywardness.[13]

To supplement his income Hartnett reviewed poetry for *The Irish Times* on a regular basis, and also reviewed fiction occasionally for *The Irish Press* and *Hibernia*. It was a busy time for him: 'I read these tales before a dead fire in deepest Marino. Rain and wind and the occasional whiff of the Corporation dump by the sea made a winter's night indeed wintery.'[14]

Hartnett was wary of the attractions of a permanent job. As he put it himself, 'if I stay long enough in the place they will want me to be a supervisor and then the trap will snap shut'.[15] He had a cautious attitude to all forms of employment that took him away from what he perceived as his vocation:

Poems have to be written, perhaps a novel and he finds he has no time. He looks around the office, or whatever, and panics: no one is interested in beauty. He finds himself betrayed into subscribing towards a pension, something utterly useless, by then he is sure to be famous, or dead. If he is young he is sure society owes him a debt. But he gets out. And is rewarded with cold and hunger and a mad gallop to find the money he got so easily, while employed within society. Society, once he stays in will give him everything – except time.[16]

The jobs he had taken, postman or night telephonist, were those where he was left alone and had time for contemplation.

In 1969 New Writers' Press, an imprint set up by his old college acquaintants, Michael Smith and Trevor Joyce, published *The Hag of Beare,* a rendition of an old Irish poem. As Michael Smith recalled:

> As far as I can make out, Michael Hartnett's translations were given to me sometime in 1969 and my intention was to bring out the entire small group of hand-written texts he gave me. Probably because of lack of resources, we settled for doing just 'The Hag of Beare' which appeared in 1969 in a hand-printed edition of 100 copies.[17]

The blurb outlined the translator's intentions: 'an attempt has been made by interlocking assonance and by alliteration, to convey something of the rhythms of the original'.

Having only just started up, the New Writers' Press was a less celebrated operation than The Dolmen Press, which had been in existence since 1951. According to Trevor Joyce, who was involved from the beginning, it was set up in conscious opposition to Liam Miller's venture. 'Dolmen Press favoured … the book as art-object rather than as a cheap, fast, and effective means of getting poetry before its prospective public.'[18] Money was raised by using the presents from Joyce's twenty-first birthday as collateral. 'After several false starts we at last laid hands on an Adana hand-press, whose salesman warned us that it could be used to print dance tickets and raffle tickets but definitely not books.' It operated under severe financial constraints, essentially surviving from book to book, and royalties were not paid: 'The money shortage prevents the Press from paying its authors; it gives books instead.' There were few overheads and no paid staff. Joyce recalled one Dickensian incident:

> I believe it was over the Christmas of 1969 that we sat around the table in Mike's unheated kitchen, dressed in scarves, hats and over-coats, setting monotype with numb fingers for the union rulebook of a Dublin hotel. Everything was undertaken communally: editing, setting, printing, making tea and sandwiches.[19]

In the beginning their printing was primitive. Joyce remembered that, on one occasion, 'the text of some of his poems had to be modified due to the shortage of certain letters in their cases of type'.[20] They also produced the poetry magazine *The Lace Curtain*. As Smith put it: 'Poetry magazines, anywhere, have, like butterflies, an all too short life; and in our mean Irish climate this brief span is even more curtailed.' It managed without any state funding in the beginning; a fact Smith made a virtue of in a letter to *The Irish Times* in 1969: 'We have survived, and are proud to have survived, without receiving a single penny from our national Farce Council.'[21] Interestingly, *The Lace Curtain* received some support from Irish-American politician Paul Dwyer and the New York Irish Institute.

Smith went on to appeal in the letter to the Irish literary public:

> So far we have been printing on a very small press that devoured our time and energy without giving us a commensurate result. With this press it would be almost impossible to go on. We now have a chance to acquire a printing machine that would … But, as has so often been said, poetry doesn't pay and we are presently broke … I am asking for 100 people to subscribe £1 each to a purchase fund for this printing machine … We have faith that there are 100 people in Ireland who think our work worth supporting …'[22]

The appeal raised £110, including £10 from Douglas Gageby, editor of *The Irish Times*, and an electric-powered printing press was purchased.

In 1971, New Writers' Press published *Selected Poems*. According to Hartnett, the reason he changed publishers was because Liam Miller was unhappy with some of the poems in the 'Notes on my Contemporaries' sequence: 'It began as a book that was to be my second book from The Dolmen Press but it never came to fruition. There were a few poems in it that Liam Miller didn't like.'[23]

In spite of his earlier stance, by 1971 Smith wasn't too proud to accept from the Arts Council a grant of £100 towards the outlay on Hartnett's *Selected Poems*. The book cost £250 to print.[24] There was a large backlog of poems by Hartnett which had appeared in various magazines, *Poetry Ireland*, *Arena*, *Kilkenny Magazine*, *The Holy Door*, etc. that had not been collected into one volume; a decade's worth of material, though not all of them were of high quality. Despite this, some people saw the title as betraying a certain arrogance for such a young poet. They felt that *Collected Poems* would have been more accurate and more modest.

Selected Poems received a less than warm welcome in some quarters. Ulsterman, James Simmons, never a fan of New Writers' Press, was as forthright as ever:

We tend to speak dismissively of Southern Irish poets in the North, being, quite reasonably, so pleased with ourselves; but it would be a pity to let this harden into a prejudice. His publisher in a typically aggressive blurb says, 'This book of poems needs no sales-talk. By his Irish contemporaries Michael Hartnett, since his early appearances in *Poetry Ireland* and *Arena*, has been acknowledged a master ... he is a poet of at least equal stature ... to Montague and Kinsella'. The word 'master' strikes me as pretentious. There is a tendency in Dublin to overvalue poetry, and for those who write poetry to feel they have some special right to despise other people. It is not a matter of speaking salutary and bitter truths, but of initiating a sort of literary gang-warfare. Hartnett has some element of pretentiousness in his poetry, stating truisms with a sort of euphonious intensity …

He is a young writer of promise. I don't think any one of the poems in this selection completely succeeds because there is an imbalance between the portentous intensity of the diction and the rather thin content and not quite achieved imagery … here is a poet to be watched. It is a talent in the balance. The arty, obscure, pretentious side might easily destroy the humility, the humanity and humour, especially if his publisher encourages him to think of himself as 'a master' and involves him in the gang-warfare of competing literary reputations. With luck, however, he might become one of the modest band whose new volumes one looks forward to with some excitement.[25]

However, compared to the review in *The Irish Press*, Simmons was positively encouraging. Vernon Scannell was stern in his opinion of it:

We are all tired of the poetry reviewer who looks at a new book as if he were a doctor examining a patient, not interested in the parts that are healthy, vigorous and well-formed, but only in the malfunctioning and diseased, the bits that should be cut out or treated so that they no longer resemble their former miserable selves. This reviewer gives all his attention to the sick parts of the volume before him, ignoring the healthy main body as of no interest to him. But what is the other kind of reviewer to do – the man who approaches the book more like a lover, hoping to find great pleasure in and give thankful praise to the body as a whole and ignore its minor imperfections – what does he do when he is faced with a collection that has almost nothing of strength and shapeliness to offer him?[26]

Scannell went on to list his misgivings:

> There are a few signs here and there of a slight but real talent, but on the whole the collection is pretentious and often banal. There is an unattractive earnestness about many of these verses, a portentousness that seems to promise epiphanies that never emerge ... What is lacking in these poems, quite apart from craft, is subject matter. You feel that most of them have their origin in the wish to write a poem rather than in common extra-literary experience and when his themes are the perennial romantic ones of love and death he seems only to decorate the abstractions rather than embody the realities ... The blurb claims that he is of 'at least equal stature to Thomas Kinsella and John Montague'. Not by my tape-measure, he's not.[27]

So negative was this review that fellow poet Brian Lynch, who had published Hartnett in his magazine *The Holy Door*, wrote to *The Irish Press* to defend his friend, setting off a short flurry of correspondence in the Letters page of the paper. Lynch accused Scannell of doing 'the poet an injustice and your readers a disservice' in his review, and concluded that:

> the sad thing is that some of your readers may have been put off buying a fine book. A sadder thing, I suppose, is that Mr Scannell has made a fool of himself in public. An apology might redeem some of the damages?[28]

Scannell wrote back from Dorset refusing to back away from his original review.

Eavan Boland in *The Irish Times* was more positive. The book could be warmly recommended not just for the grace and violence of 'a phrase, an image, a perspective', but also:

his obvious confidence in the precision of the lyric form, its ability to turn a thought, a heartbreak, a memory, on a sixpence – pays off handsomely ... One would not have to know Irish poetry in its heritage and language, to detect in Michael Hartnett's own work the strength that his knowledge on and his interpretations of the Gaelic tradition has endowed his work in the English language, as shown in these poems.[29]

Boland concluded her review with a prediction:

Michael Hartnett, with his knowledge of the Irish tradition, his imaginative access through true talent into the English tradition, may face two roads. The distinction of his poetry suggests that he could even construct a highway through them, thus ending their division.[30]

James Liddy, in a private letter to Michael Smith of New Writers' Press, echoed Boland's views:

Your Hartnett book is the best thing you have done. Important. The selection is good, with the first haunting poems, the voluptuous Madrid offerings ... Michael has powerful old magic, dark & primitive poems ... The unchanging poems, and his talk about craftsmanship reveal him as really Gaelic. The zeal for metre and syllable is a hand down from the bards. He belongs to several centuries and in this pure state has rarely got into English.[31]

In 1972, New Writers' Press published Hartnett's 'Tao' in book form. According to Trevor Joyce, New Writers' Press, 'negotiated with Hartnett for permission to bring out his version of the 'Tao', first published in *Arena*. He eventually acceded in exchange for a promise of a pint of stout for each of its seventy-odd sections.'[32]

It got tepid reviews. Tom McGurk in *The Irish Times* was dismissive. He did not see the point of the translation, since Hartnett knew no Chinese and he felt that there was little of the poet himself in the finished work and that, in general, 'the whole thing seems a rather expensive piece of homework'.[33]

In response, Hartnett and Richard Ryan wrote to the paper, ostensibly to complain about the unsympathetic appraisal of Valentin Iremonger in the same review (Ryan was Iremonger's editor at The Dolmen Press). The two of them did not feel they had to defend Iremonger's reputation. Rather, they wished to express their 'amazement at the standards of editorial judgement … which should permit such uncomprehending and total dismissal of his work'.[34] No mention of McGurk's opinion of Hartnett's 'Tao' was made.

The literary editor, Terence De Vere White, made the connection and wrote in reply:

> Mr Tom McGurk in the review in question was rather dismissive of Mr Hartnett's book. It would have perhaps been well for Mr Hartnett to have mentioned this. If I send books to a reviewer I do not think I should question his judgements. Very often they conflict with my own.[35]

Hartnett dispatched another epistle: 'I should like to point out that I do not and did not object to Mr McGurk's opinion of my book.' He went on to state that personally he did not think that 'Tao' was one of his best poems, flatly contradicting what New Writers' Press had written in the blurb of their edition:

> I certainly agree with the Literary Editor that the judgements of reviewers should not be questioned by him; a book may receive a 'good'

or 'bad' review, but there is a new and insidious type of journalism coming into being in which books are condemned without a show of evidence for or against. Mr McGurk was certainly guilty of this practice in his non-review … I think an editor is entitled, even bound, to object …[36]

There the matter rested until Tom McGurk became involved again. Once the fur and feathers had settled he put pen to paper:

I gather from the refreshing and lilting breezes of fresh air blowing through these correspondence columns, once again, that the beery interruptions of Messrs Hartnett and Ryan have ended. I apologise to the public at large for this influx of Dublin literary pub squabbling into their most excellent newspaper. If I have unfairly treated Valentin Iremonger, I will see to it in my own way. However, in his immortal words, 'I will not indulge their arrogance any longer'.

I received the Messer's attack with pain and pleasure. Pain, that they singled this one out of the fifty-odd I have reviewed for *The Irish Times* this past year, for attack; and pleasure that they did it so badly. To safeguard my honour I have decided to challenge the Messers to a duel. Since such honourable practices are outside both State and Church Law, I intend to fulfil my challenge in the one part of Ireland free of repressive authority, Free Derry. The Honourable Gentleman, Mr Ben Kiely of Tyrone has graciously consented to be my second. I will appear with him at Free Derry Corner stripped to the waist at midday, on Wednesday the 12th of July, 1972. I expect the Messers to turn up and account for themselves.[37]

McGurk added:

It should be noted that I am a distant relation of the famous 'Muscles' McGurk, the strongest employee of Guinness' who was known to have exercised himself nakedly, and with great vigour, in the Phoenix Park, in the early part of this century.

Despite this contretemps, Hartnett remained the principal poetry reviewer for *The Irish Times* in the early 1970s. He also contributed other articles on literary matters to the paper and continued to review for *The Irish Press* and *Hibernia* magazine. And, like most of the poets in Dublin at the time, readings of his work became a useful source of revenue.

9

'Till, Talk and Tankard'

As Anthony Cronin described it sardonically in 'The Great Poetry Boom, 1970s', it was supposed to be a good time for poetry in Dublin, even though Cronin did not seem convinced:

Yeats, Yeats, Yeats, Yeats
Clarke, Clarke, Clarke, Clarke,
Kavanagh, Kavanagh, Kavanagh
… these we know are the true greats

Not forgetting, 'Kinsella, Kinsella, Kinsella …

Poetry readings were a widespread feature of literary life in Dublin in the late 1960s. Poets who wished to publicise their works were required to be performers as well as writers. James Liddy outlined the background to such readings in an article in the *Kilkenny Magazine*:

There are certain trade union regulations about verse readings which most poets support. The only persons allowed to read are the poet himself, and possibly someone he has personally trained. The poems must be read rhythmically in their native voice, with respect for each verse unit and for the line. No genuine poet tolerates some fool of an actor reading his work, even if this is sometimes amusing.

… The poet is neither an entertainer nor, in the end, a teacher. His true aim, besides writing poems, is to discover himself, to fit into his true mask ... The poet must be careful to disdain. He must do, as a matter of duty, everything to its finish: he must laugh until he cries, he must drink until he gets drunk. He must grow more alive as he grows older, and he must die just as he becomes alive. Finally, he must never, in any circumstances, put any of his life in the bank. It is for what he is, as much as what he says, that the audience comes into the room.[1]

Whatever the reasons, poetry readings became more popular in Dublin at the tail end of the 1960s, and were often combined with music recitals. This boom enabled poets like Hartnett to make a certain amount of money from readings, but it was not always a comfortable way of making a few bob. Eavan Boland reported on a reading by three poets in the Project Arts Centre in 1971 with an entrance fee of twenty pence, 'less than half the price of a packet of cigarettes and far better for your constitution' as she put it. She was critical of the amateur organisation, a late start, and 'the phone rang and was answered conversationally while one of the readings was in progress'.[2]

Hayden Murphy accompanied Hartnett and Pearse Hutchinson to a reading in Cavan and 'was reduced to a nervous wreck by Michael Hartnett's continuous punning, an art form at which he is not only adept, but ruthless'.

On arriving at their destination they were 'ushered through a meal', then they encountered their audience:

We sat and stared ... Ladies all, with a conspicuous priest sitting towards the back between two nuns. Later we were joined by several more males supporting a jocular comrade whose bout of heckling repartee with Pearse Hutchinson was most effective, if not entertaining. We read, and apart from the aforementioned gentleman, were politely received. The priest nodded sympathetically at the nun on his left, and several of the ladies blushed discreetly at one of Pearse's more vigorous pieces, but otherwise all was well … However, the next morning was not such a merry occasion and after a day of intermittent attempts at thumbing a lift on a very wet day on a very quiet road we fell back on to the evening bus.[3]

Even in their Dublin stronghold these poets had a tough time. Roy Lisker, an American writer, was struck by the liveliness and quarrelsome nature of the literary pubs of Dublin:

Certain cities, such as San Francisco, Paris and Dublin, have earned a reputation as literary centres. Among these, it is probably easier to uncover the literary scene in Dublin than anywhere else. The scene tends to gravitate, as most things in Dublin do, around a small number of mead-halls centrally located around St Stephen's Green and off Grafton Street. Thus in a typical afternoon in McDaid's one will usually find that the percentage of poets to relatively ordinary people is rather high, compared to that in the general population, or in most pubs for that matter. In McDaid's it is easy enough to meet them, not that difficult to drink with them, and patience can sometimes be rewarded with an actual conversation. However, one should be warned in advance that to mention the subject of poetry is to enter as an infidel into the places of the elect. It is wise not to do so right off, if ever.[4]

And when not writing the poets still kept busy:

When the poets are not talking or sulking in McDaid's they are usually writing poetry; between times they have been able to organise several poetry events, the most notable of which are the weekly Thursday night readings in the lounge above Sinnott's bar, on King

St just off Grafton. Whether Left bank or Right, Underground or Establishment, the Sinnott's readings are unquestionably central to the literary scene in Ireland … The Sinnott's readings are scheduled to begin at 8.30 but this has tended to shift more and more to somewhere between 9.15 and 9.30. As a result the lounge is virtually empty until 9.00 but becomes packed solid by 9.30 … One will frequently find Pearse Hutchinson sitting by the doorway, collecting the half-crown admission which will later be divided up between the participants. The function of master of ceremonies will frequently be taken by Hayden Murphy, a young avant-garde poet, who with his many contacts with the English and Continental literary scene is well qualified for the job … There is quite a contrast between the two, Hutchinson and Murphy; the first something of an aged bard, dreamy, immersed in the silence of wisdom; the other with the impudent manner of a young rebel, ready to spar on any pretext, however irrelevant.[5]

Lisker, a poet himself, described the robust nature of the proceedings:

Since poetry at Sinnott's is a living art one can well imagine that things can become pretty lively there. Because of the large audience, the continual clanging of the cash register (as drinks are served all through the readings, much to the annoyance of almost everyone except the bartender) and because opinions about poetry tend to be of a passionate nature, it is rare that one can expect to find here the tranquil atmosphere in which poetry should be read to be properly appreciated.

The crowd showed little patience towards those they did not appreciate: 'Last month … a poet struggling to be heard against a background of chatter and insolent remarks, had to stop twice to ask for silence.'

Lisker asked 'a wispy-bearded intellectual' next to him why he insisted on talking while poetry was being read. 'If I thought,' he sneered, 'that a single line of that trash was worth listening to, I would have shut up long ago.'

Not every writer was impressed by such activities. Michael Smith, in his role as editor of *The Lace Curtain*, wrote:

> In recent years poetry has tended to be treated by pub-owners, organisers of theatre festivals and fund-raisers of all kinds as a profitable, if not very profitable, gimmick. Many poets, all too eager for any recognition of their utility in a utility-minded society, and appreciative of the pittances doled out to them as payment for their entertainment services, have acquiesced in this degradation of poetry to the level of amusement, cultural titillation and commercial gimmick … Poetry readings are fine when they are simply that, the poetry read and listened to for its own sake. Poetry is not a carnival side-show. The public must either accept or reject it on its own terms, and the poets who want fame and money had much better take up ballad singing, for which many young Irish poets seem to be more suitably qualified, both by talent and aspiration.[6]

Such was Smith's dislike of the trend he vowed, in an article in *The Irish Times*, not to do any more readings in Sinnott's. He conceded that the readings 'on rare occasions' could be entertaining:

> but the poetry is too often lost amid the din of till, talk and tankard … On the credit side … for the poets reading, Sinnott's … provides the means and occasion for a few jars and an excuse for a little vain self-display at the expense of the poetry.[7]

Not surprisingly, Smith's article provoked Leland Bardwell, Eiléan

Ní Chuilleanáin, and Hayden Murphy to take to the letters page of *The Irish Times* to defend the readings in Sinnott's.

While Sinnott's may have been at the rowdier end of the scale, most readings were sedate. At one such recital Nell McCafferty of *The Irish Times* kept her eye on the audience as much as the performer:

> 'Rosa sits moaning at the gate, her hacked off breasts before her on a plate,' declaimed Michael Hartnett, in the carpeted dimness of the National Gallery lecture theatre ... He was reading his own translation of Lorca ... Listening to him were 52 people, scattered comfortably along the empty rows of soft leather seating, in the quiet hall buried below the weekend revelling. In an audience composed mainly of young be-jeaned girls and single well-dressed women, a man in evening dress, his little daughter by his side, added the right touch of casual culture. There were five couples.[8]

Hartnett had used his visits to Spain to help him to translate the gypsy ballads of the renowned Spanish poet and dramatist Lorca. He preferred Lorca's more lyrical early works to his more surrealistic poems and told Dennis O'Driscoll some years later:

> I went to Spain in 1964, deliberately to learn Spanish so that I could translate Lorca. He was able, up to his visit to the States, to handle and subdue the surrealistic wave that was breaking over Europe, without going verbally mad. He did go mad in the verbal sense in his long diatribe, 'The Poet in New York'. It's an extraordinary book; but I parted company with him then, verbally.[9]

According to Rosemary Hartnett, she translated the ballads into:

English prose and Michael rendered it into poetry ... It is true to say that Michael did have a great facility with the Romance languages, probably because of his knowledge of Latin and his ear for language but he was not fluent enough to translate Lorca.[10]

Hartnett's occasional visits to Spain ended when he had a run-in with the authorities:

Michael finally left Spain as a fugitive due to a run-in with the police in Madrid. He had been unwise enough to make several attempts to meet with a Spanish poet who was a political prisoner. The regime maintained he was not in jail. Then for the second time Michael was stopped on the street for being drunk and for not carrying identification. The Guardia Civil accompanied him to his lodgings and confiscated his passport. Fortunately Michael went to the Irish Embassy the next day for advice and on hearing his story they advised him to leave the country forthwith and gave him the necessary documentation to do so. He hurriedly took their advice and spent the train journey to the Spanish border hunched into his overcoat, heart pounding at the sight of a uniform. Thankfully the documents provided got him through.[11]

Hartnett was perhaps too reticent to ever become an accomplished performer. Máire Ní Fhrighil of *The Irish Times* described Hartnett at an event 'in the comfortable disorder of the Council Chamber in the City Hall', where 'unfortunately a microphone was not available and it was sometimes difficult to catch a phrase'. Despite this, the reporter was impressed by the poet's translations of Lorca, which 'simulated the rhyming patterns of the originals, and very evidently have captured their exotic mood, rich and exciting as colossal stained-glass windows'.[12]

John Boland of *The Irish Press* was of similar opinion: 'Mr

Hartnett is a fine and sincere poet, if a rather muted reader. And I feel that poetry readings should be judged on their dramatic qualities, rather than on the intrinsic quality of the poetry.'[13]

However, one of Hartnett's readings did turn out to be quite dramatic, though not through anything the poet himself did. The Imperial Hotel in Dundalk had to be evacuated during one of his readings as a result of a bomb warning – it turned out to be a hoax.

In 1973 Goldsmith Press published Hartnett's *Gypsy Ballads*; yet another change of publisher for him. Goldsmith Press was run on Saturdays by Desmond Egan from his brother's garage in Castleknock. During the week he taught in Newbridge Secondary School, but he 'was interested purely in poetry … it's my main interest in life – I muddle and mess at everything else, but getting words on the page, getting results …'[14]

Egan and Hartnett had worked together on *Choice*, a representative collection of verse by contemporary Irish poets. The choice of poem was left to the poet, who added a short commentary. It wasn't necessarily the poet's best work, but instead the one the poet liked best. The production process was not without its difficulties. Egan recalled how he had to throw away '15,000 sheets of paper when they were cut all different sizes by mistake'. Egan had experienced such 'time-wasting, foot-dragging, getting-nowhere treatment at the hands of others when he tried to have a collection issued that he decided to do it himself'.[15] It was called Goldsmith Press because the Egans came from Athlone, and had a high regard for Oliver Goldsmith.

10

'EXQUISITE DREAM OF A POET'

The late 1960s was a lively time in Dublin. As John Montague put it, 'you couldn't shove a load of coal into a basement without disturbing an avant-garde play'.[1] This was the environment in which Hartnett struggled to make a name for himself, yet he was no innocent when it came to his literary line of business and was aware of the cliques and fashions that shaped a poet's career. 'Lack of quality is no bar to publication if the writer is compatible to the editor in personality and sect'[2] and he was not impressed with much of the poetry being produced by his contemporaries in Dublin:

> A lot of poetry that is being published nowadays is very loose in structure – it is talking poetry, public platform poetry, you can speak it loudly, shout it out. But the difference between my idea of an Irish tradition and the English tradition is that Irish poetry, classic Gaelic poetry, is more difficult to achieve as form than English poetry. English poetry, for me, is simple to write. I could write a sonnet now for you and structure-wise it may be fine, but Irish poets at the moment – a lot of them are despairing of the looseness, the free verse, the Ginsberg type of poetry.[3]

In 1971 *The Irish Times* ran a series of articles which they called 'The Closed Circuit', in which they asked a number of writers to express their views on the narrow world of Irish – and especially Dublin – literary life. Hartnett, Eavan Boland and Michael Smith contributed. Unsurprisingly, Hartnett was disparaging in his conclusions. He did not enjoy what passed for socialising in the Dublin literary scene:

> I have been acquainted with 'literary circles' in Dublin since 1962 and have sat for hours in pubs and learned nothing about poetry. I have learnt that envy is the highest form of emotion that the pub-poet mentality can achieve: I have learnt that 'literary pubs' are schools for the most wearying, boring, pathetic conversationalists. I have learnt that 'cliques' comprise at best one or two good poets and a commonality of poseurs and downright impostors.
>
> I have seen poets puke their guts out night after night, wallowing in a false and unwilling fellowship in an effort not to offend. I have heard hysterical young men and spiteful old men scream at each other, not because of the debasement of poetry which should be their main concern, but over a false and illusionary jockeying for monopoly.
>
> A buyer of copious rounds can win the heart of any poet, can be elected to the most closed of closed shops: a fraud, who with a surface knowledge of literary history and who can write and publish his polite (and impolite) meaningless phrases may be considered openly the peer of better poets though he is privately and immediately dismissed by them for what he is: but he is tolerated and freely stamps with glee on the body of poetry.

Hartnett felt that the creation of poetry was not a public act: 'Poetry, like copulation or defecation, is essentially a private rite.' He had a lofty disdain for most of his fellow practitioners:

> There is a decadent thread in Dublin literary life, a casual sloppy

school of bad prose writers who think that because their lines reach only halfway across a page they are poets: they are mainly fostered in the pubs where loneliness dare not allow the loss of one enemy of poetry because it would mean the loss of one personal friend. That a constant reassurance is needed by true poets from such minions is a tragedy. A poet needs the company of poets, but all are not Goldsmiths who glisten. He must then take them as he finds them: he must also suffer their surroundings, their acolytes, their stupidities.[4]

Hartnett concluded that:

poets have the edge and can survive by the narrowest of margins; it is, however, this surviving that can break the spirit and purge true poetry out of mind … a poet must be a man as solitary and secret as the act of poetry itself.

Michael Smith was also disapproving of the scene in the capital in the 1970s:

At least while *Arena*, *Poetry Ireland* and Patrick Kavanagh were alive, I was aware of a literary life in Dublin. Maybe it wasn't much, judged by that of New York or Paris or London; but its very presence in a society still, in the early 1960s, desperately scrabbling at the greasy till, gave an assurance and sustenance to the young poet without which, his survival, for any length of time, would have been very doubtful. That such literary life exists now, I am not so sure.[5]

Smith believed that McDaid's had become a skeleton of its former self. It was now no more than 'an uncomfortable pub', even if still the local of a number of poets, 'being central and recollect of old memories'. In fact, most of the literary clientele decamped from McDaid's when it was sold in 1972. Its legendary barman Paddy O'Brien made an attempt to buy it but was outbid at the auction and Tommy Smith of Grogan's offered Paddy a job at his premises instead. Smith outlined what happened next. 'He accepted and immediately his club of friends followed. Like the Pied Piper, he led them across the former car park where the Westbury Hotel now stands and business resumed as normal.'[6]

Grogan's became Hartnett's regular haunt. Hugh McFadden recalled meeting Hartnett in the pub in the mid-1970s:

> Pleasant memories remain … of 'alternative' afternoons or evenings in his company in Grogan's along with Mr Jordan and others … Hayden Murphy arriving in with a duffel-bag full of copies of the latest 'Broadsheet' magazine … the artists, Charlie Cullen, Charlie Brady and Paddy Graham having esoteric discussions about the drawing of one good unbroken 'line'.[7]

Michael Smith acknowledged that:

> Dublin is supposed to be notorious for its cliques. At its best, a clique is a perfectly natural grouping of people with common interests; at its worst, it is an attempt to monopolise power. As editor of *The Lace Curtain* and of a small poetry press, I have been accused of being the kernel of a literary clique in the bad sense. Being a Dubliner, I accept the inevitability of the charge, but I would like to put it down here that I have always been consciously opposed to cliques in the bad sense I have defined and that when I find myself rejecting work because I do not happen to like the personality of the writer, I will immediately abandon editing and publishing.[8]

Eavan Boland took a different tack:

When a group of young poets meet in that casual yet close relationship which is ever after vulnerable to being termed a clique; when they discover the simple delight of shouting one another down in terms of life or literature; when moreover they make warm, personal friendships concurrently, then they are afterwards termed a clique – or, more vulgarly, backscratchers ... I would prefer to think that they become in their collective capacity, an intractable, puzzling object like an uncut diamond. But diamonds, like literary cliques, possess potentially as many facets as can be discovered ... Cliques cannot make poets or poetry, but they can provide a climate in which artistic endowments can thrive or perish.[9]

John Jordan was of a similar opinion, feeling that poets in Dublin tended to be categorised as one kind or the other. 'These bracketings are artificial and often motivated by jealousy and malice, for the Dublin literary village is a beery and bloody one ... I pat myself on the back for my own (much imperilled) immunity to coteries.'[10]

Hartnett could be scathing in his opinion of his fellow poets, as is evident from a spat he had with *Broadsheet* editor Hayden Murphy. *Broadsheet* was an eclectic magazine, published occasionally and sold mainly by Murphy himself going from pub to pub, though bookshops like Parsons, Eblana and Hodges Figgis also stocked copies. As Hayden Murphy explained:

In February 1967 with *Poetry Ireland* temporarily silenced, I made a brief effort to fill the gap. Together with Benedict Ryan, another young poet silenced in emigration, we conceived and gave birth to *Broadsheet*, an anarchic genesis between a magazine and a poster in form, and the traditional with the avant-garde in material ... To fail because of being over-ambitious is far more rewarding than succeeding mediocrity.[11]

At ten pence an issue, this worked out at less than one pence a poem. Murphy still tried to pay each contributor a fee. Unsurprisingly, *Broadsheet* generally ran at a loss.

Many of its issues carried editorials that were written by Murphy 'in the shadow of penury', as he put it, as he kept his readership up-to-date with the saga of his dealings with the Arts Council. *Broadsheet* was forever on the brink of disaster, and there were often long gaps between publications. In 1968, Murphy told *The Irish Times*: 'Now it lies financially crippled, diseased with debt but ever-willing to re-appear if necessary or able'.[12] The Arts Council did not provide consistent financial backing, although it did give support to some issues. This intermittent support only seemed to enrage Murphy.

Broadsheet 11 hit the streets and the pubs in May 1971. By then, the Arts Council had stopped their grant to the magazine. In his editorial, Murphy commented, 'I thank them for what they have done, and condemn them for what they are failing to do, for literature in Ireland.'[13] The Arts Council found an unusual backer in this instance. A more than usually waspish Hartnett, in *The Irish Times* review section, took a swing at the magazine and the poetry of its editor:

Unlike the last *Broadsheet* this is a one-sheet affair, some of the usual rubbish has been jettisoned (pages of printer's frolics and comic-book illustrations) and if the Arts Council are responsible for the size of the current issue, and therefore for the cutting of its gangrenous limbs, they are to be congratulated. The usual coat of pornography has also been wiped off by the frugality of the Arts Council, but the comic-book illustrations still manage to survive … In this cleaner, tidier issue what is good can be seen quite clearly; what is bad can also be seen, no longer hidden by the usual ballast which can charitably be described as eccentric.

Having praised a select few of the contributions Hartnett went back on the attack:

> The bad unfortunately outnumber the good, 10-to-6; these are not utterly bad except for two but what is good enough for *Broadsheet* is not always a poet's best efforts … Hayden Murphy's 'Thanks' is another of his abortive attempts to translate his thoughts into that elusive medium, English … I have no doubt that Hayden Murphy's head is full of poems, but the credibility gap becomes wide indeed when he struggles with the hydra of the English language.[14]

Murphy, predictably, took offence and wrote about it in his editorial in the next issue of *Broadsheet*:

> As for the Arts Council, they still leave the literary arts in financial poverty … Pictures can be hung but poets and writers make untidy corpses … To praise them, on any grounds, for doing this is evil and destructive and is an inexcusable way of making a critical point.[15]

He then referred to Hartnett – though not by name – as 'a critic who is becoming infamous for philosophical inaccuracy and pedanticism'.

Hartnett retaliated, in turn, in *The Irish Times*:

> I suppose I shall have to reply to Hayden Murphy's coy 'editorial' … I cannot find where philosophy (inaccurate or otherwise) has entered into any review I have written: I must more or less corroborate the second charge – of 'pedanticism' – by saying that there is no such word … The editor seems to have misunderstood what I said about the Arts Council. I will now re-state it as simply as I can, for his benefit: I praise the Arts Council for withdrawing its grant from

Broadsheet and from *Broadsheet* only. It forced the editor to curb his unselective abandon in choosing inane material for what is otherwise a good production.

In his 'editorial' he further delivers this pompous and clumsily-made sentence: 'Unfortunately he will be incapable of ever being a competent critic until he learns the art of constructive criticism.' This is apparently in reply to my statement that he cannot write the English language: Well, I do employ constructive criticism – whenever I see promise and hope. While he attempts to muddle through with a profusion of abstract words hoping to bring off the triumph of mind over metre, while he ignores the fact that there is also an area of constructive English, I can see neither promise nor hope in or for his work.[16]

It is indicative of Hartnett's charm or perhaps of Hayden Murphy's forgiving nature that future editions of *Broadsheet* included works by Hartnett. As Murphy wrote to Hartnett in later life, 'I remember with affection even our rows ...'[17]

In the next edition, Murphy was back lambasting the Arts Council, 'And yet again I moan about the niggardly treatment of the literary arts by the patronisingly named (by the inept artisans of power) Arts Council ...'[18]

In 1972, Elgy Gillespie of *The Irish Times* gave a description of Murphy's working methods:

For as long as anyone under thirty can remember there has been Hayden Murphy. For as long as anyone can remember he has worn an elderly donkey-jacket and drunk in his editorial seat in the intensive section at the back of McDaid's, Harry Street. And for the past three and a half years odd he has taken a duffel-bag to the streets of Dublin, selling *Broadsheet*, the poetry sheet he collects, selects, corrects (his wife does the typing, edits, layouts, Louis Clear

prints it on Quikprint for him), touts and flogs. A one-poet band …
Broadsheet is now into its fifteenth issue, and has at least succeeded in
its primary aim; that of keeping Hayden thinly alive.[19]

After a quick 'livener' in Kehoe's, Gillespie did the rounds of the
pubs with the poet, even venturing into Davy Byrne's on his behalf,
as Murphy was barred from there. Murphy was 'wearing his poor-
but-worthy look and fiddling with his dejected duffel-bag'.

'Twenty-nine poems for ten pence' was Murphy's main selling
point as he did his tour. 'You could always use it for bog-paper, or
make *papier-mâché* ashtrays,' someone told them. 'True,' Murphy
conceded, 'it makes good wall-paper as well.'[20]

By 1974, and *Broadsheet* 20, Murphy had virtually given up
looking for state aid. He intended to produce a larger issue for a
bumper twenty-first birthday edition.

> This will entail cash. May I now … appeal to some of our commercial
> firms to arise with suggestions of a monetary nature. At this stage I
> usually haul in the Arts Council but now, having financed with help
> from friends the last ten issues, I know that they are contemptible in
> relation to literature.[21]

In June 1974, the bumper birthday edition did appear, costing a
massive fifty pence. Murphy was in vintage form:

> May I thank the Arts Council for their past interest in my demise,
> and hope that they notice that I have not forgotten to mention them.
> At date of going to press … they have yet to decide if I am eligible for
> some of their booty … I have survived 21 issues with no help from
> them since number 10. Accountant I am not, angry at their petty
> bureaucracy I am.[22]

Having said all that, however, he ended with the heartfelt plea: 'Nonetheless I will be more than grateful if they will give me the applied-for financial help towards this issue.' He thanked the contributors over the years and hoped that they would all enjoy a pint in Heaven. 'I will try and arrange for an indexed slate to be set up for those of the more angelic spirits.'

It was a common complaint of the editors of literary magazines that they could not rely on state funding. That some magazines could get backing and others couldn't was the cause of much resentment. Brian Lynch's *The Holy Door* had the lament: 'No thanks are due to the Arts Council for producing this issue. *Poetry Ireland*, *The Dublin Magazine*, the *Kilkenny Magazine*, etc. all qualify in that direction. What have they got that we haven't?'[23] *The Lace Curtain* could be said to have taken pride in its lack of state support, though Smith was not too proud to accept Arts Council funding when it became available.

Hartnett became involved in a number of squabbles in his capacity of reviewer. He had an abrasive turn of phrase. When he assessed 'I, in the Membership of my Days' by fellow Limerick man, actor Richard Harris, in *Hibernia*, he made no allowances for any fellowship:

Richard Harris wrestled with his ego in this collection and his ego won. It is difficult to take an actor's verse seriously. Is it a genuine attempt of a tormented intellect to express itself or is this just a hard-fisted, hard-loving, hard-drinking Irish actor hoping to be that most desirable of all beings, a hard-fisted, hard-loving, hard-drinking Irish poet? He does not succeed in either case. He wavers between the naïve and the obscure … The lack of punctuation, the haphazard line breaks, make what this book contains look like poetry, and I am sure that, if delivered by an actor it would sound like poetry. The abandonment of formal verse made the composition of poetry seem easy and within the power of any literate person … He seems to ignore or not to know that the single, essential qualification required to write poetry, major or minor, is to be a poet first and anything one has to be after.[24]

Hartnett's stern criticism could create enemies, though this did not seem to overly bother him.

When poetry suffers, names should be named: certain editors, mock-poets and critics should be pilloried, spat upon. I am on the side of art, of mainstream poetry. I would rather that true poetry was respected, read and written and not have a friend to my name, than see it gutted, counterfeited and mocked and be the centre of a bright table for the rest of my life.[25]

He made no concessions, even to minor poets. In an *Irish Times* review he referred to Diana Tomkin as 'a poet-as-defined-by-the-*Reader's Digest*' and stated that her concepts 'in general are trite, precious and house-wifely'.[26] Hartnett's use of the term 'house-wifely' provoked a number of letters to *The Irish Times*, calling him patronising and insulting.

Even when he approved of a poet, Hartnett's judgements could be harsh:

Alice Curtayne has written an interesting account of an uninteresting life. Francis Ledwidge was killed at thirty. He lived most of his years in Slane, in quiet and beautiful surroundings; he pursued his love-affairs with a singular lack of open passion; he left no great poetry behind him. Yet his life and poetry command a great affection among many people, in my case he is one of my favourite poets … she has honoured a delicate poet, whose small lyrics, though lacking depth and literary training, are at times so close to nature that they are, like many of Nature's smaller and more beautiful things, almost invisible.[27]

Such high principles could easily get a critic into trouble. Dennis O'Driscoll was aware of the difficulty of being a reviewer in a small country:

> In Ireland, the critical vacuum that quickly fills with the hot air of special pleading has one obvious source: the extreme difficulty of publishing tough-minded judgements in a country where the reviewer is liable to bump into his subject on the journey to mail the review. Critics here – as no doubt in other countries – may be divided roughly into three categories: those who are honest and eclectic; sanguine souls who detect gold in every pebble and promise in every lost cause; and finally, those who are permissive where their own coterie is concerned and dismissive of any presumption on the part of outsiders … There is plenty of mutual back-scratching as well as eye-scratching.[28]

In fact, O'Driscoll felt that:

> the problem actually, is not that the Irish Republic can be too difficult a place to establish a reputation as a poet but that it may be too easy … Those with more tenacity than talent will find magazines to publish them, radio slots to broadcast their 'thoughts for the day', arts centres to host their readings, newspapers to publicise their activities … As I know to my cost, Irish poets are apt to take grave offence at adverse criticism, however mild and well-meant …[29]

Whatever about public criticism, in private there was even more disparagement. John Montague considered that 'What prevailed in the poetic world of Dublin was acrimony and insult: a poem was to be kicked, not examined; the begrudgers ruled.'[30]

Elgy Gillespie asked Hayden Murphy:

'Why do poets allow themselves the kind of catty and doggy vendettas they do, when on the whole it is a thin but a friendly sort of a living?' Murphy replied, 'It's because in this small place it is a personality sort of thing. In England solidarity among poets is greater and they talk about technical things.'[31]

Hartnett had a simpler explanation. Mockery, he felt, was one of the main national curses of the Irish.

With a young family to support, he continued to work as a night telephonist and supplemented his income by reviewing for *The Irish Times*, *The Irish Press* and *Hibernia*. And then there were the poetry readings and occasional appearances on RTÉ radio and television. All this left was little time for writing poetry. It was a treadmill and he was unhappy with the urban life he was leading.

Michael Smith, his publisher of old, felt that Hartnett's writing had stalled by the early 1970s. In the *Denver Quarterly*, while praising his technical ability, Smith was critical of what he saw as his narrow world view:

Michael Hartnett is technically (if such a distinction is valid) the most accomplished Irish poet the better side of middle age. His poetry displays a rare mastery of language, an incredible finesse in the construction of rhythm and image, and there is certainly no Irish poet who can produce the *mot juste* as often and as successfully as Hartnett. At present, however he is still satisfied with sniping the smaller events of life, to which his style is supremely suited. But what he needs, for his growth as a poet, is to take on more intractable experience. He must know that the vitality of style depends on the willingness of the writer to start afresh each time, to be accessible to the fecund influence of the sundry of the world. Otherwise, exhaustion through repetition, boredom and death.[32]

Smith repeated his analysis in Douglas Dunn's book *Two Decades of Writing – A Critical Survey*:

> Hartnett's early work promised that he would develop into a poet considerable by any standards; but something went wrong. What Hartnett brought to poetry and what enabled him to avoid the conventional pitfalls of Irish versifying was a precision of language and image which could examine experience as deftly as a scalpel. But ... the poetry devolved into a decorative preciosity ... the style dominated and jailed the man.[33]

Nor was Hartnett happy with the condition of the country. He felt that Ireland was losing its language and with it, its identity. In February 1975 Hartnett outlined to Desmond Rushe of the *Irish Independent* his hopes and fears for the country:

> In the matter of language Michael Hartnett's ideal Ireland would be a bilingual state with English used for trade and commerce and Gaelic for dealing in such things as love and poetry and philosophy. It is an exquisite dream and it is inspired by an appreciation of Gaelic as the major element in our cultural heritage. Whether it can ever become a reality or not, Mr Hartnett has made his own decision to change over to Gaelic in his poetry writing. He is doing it not just because he finds Gaelic a beautifully rich and flexible language and the language of his ancestors but also as a protest against long-held attitudes towards the language.[34]

Desmond Rushe's 'Tatler's Parade' column was headlined 'Exquisite Dream of a Poet'.

11

'*TÁIMSE* FLABBERGASTED'

One part of his dream was about to come true. Hartnett had been anxious for some time to give up his job as telephonist in order to devote himself to writing full-time. He was also considering moving from Dublin back to County Limerick with his young family, unhappy with the literary life in the capital with its cliques and feuds. In March 1975 Hartnett was awarded £2,000 by the Irish-American Cultural Fellowship. The Irish-American Cultural Institute had been founded by Dr Eoin McKiernan, from St Paul, Minnesota, and had supported Irish writers over a number of years, in particular, writers in Irish. The Institute also made television documentaries and published the journal *Éire/Ireland*. Breandán Ó hEithir, the RTÉ journalist, was also presented with a fellowship at the same time.

At a reception in the Gresham Hotel to announce the awards, attended by the President of Ireland Cearbhall Ó Dálaigh, the president of the Irish-American Cultural Institute, Dr McKiernan, explained that the purpose of the fellowships was to enable writers to devote themselves completely to their writing during a stated period. Hartnett certainly fitted the bill.

In 1969, at a public meeting in Nenagh, McKiernan had declared that the revival of the Irish language was far too important to be left to any government because 'no government ever rises beyond mediocrity'. There were people in high places with a 'peasant mentality' who were trying to give away their birthright:

I would not like to see any language die. Every language was mean-
ingful. Living languages were not found in museums or university
offices. They were – and must be – found on the lips of people …
The whole picture of a people is to be found in its language and this
is what Ireland must retain if it is not to be nothing more than an
English province.[1]

Up until 1972, the Institute had restricted its awards to those who
wrote in the Irish language but it then departed from this policy
and included writers in English. McKiernan outlined the criteria
it used to decide its grants:

Shall writers be given awards in recognition of a standard of achievement over a period of years? Or for a single work? Or for the best
work on a set piece? For new experimental work? For the best work
in a particular genre? Or should works be commissioned, as is common enough practice in the other arts? Or should these monies be
invested in young writers of promise to provide them with a year of
travel, of study, of time for writing?[2]

These were the questions to which McKiernan admitted the Institute did not have all the answers. It was quite satisfied to be merely
an instrument in putting up the money and would not presume
how it should be used.

In a letter in September 1972, Brendan Kennelly, who was
aware of Hartnett's financial circumstances and his general un-
happiness with his lot, had suggested that he approach McKiernan:

You did not mention your response to my suggestion that you
study or work in America for a few years. You should write to Eoin

McKiernan of *Éire-Ireland*, tell him your situation and ask him for
money – enough to support you and your family.[3]

In 1972, Hartnett went on a lecture tour of the United States
under the auspices of the Irish-American Cultural Institute, as
part of an 'Irish Fortnight'.

The 1975 fellowship allowed Hartnett to leave his job as a
night telephonist and start writing full-time. However, he did
not want to give up his permanent and pensionable post entirely,
but there was a problem. According to *The Irish Press*, Hartnett
complained that the leave of absence he had sought, and that he
was entitled to from the Department of Posts and Telegraphs,
has not yet been authorised. He was looking for an unpaid leave
of absence for one year. After a certain amount of friction it was
eventually granted.

Hartnett bought a small cottage and an acre of land at Glendarragh, in Templeglantine, Limerick, not far from where he had
been reared. 'I wanted to live among my own people, but in an area
with traditional roots, which Templeglantine has,' he explained.[4]

At the time, Elgy Gillespie of *The Irish Times* described him
thus:

Michael Hartnett – self-described romantic lyricist, wit, shrewd
countryman, telephonist and member of that small, intense, nomadic
band who sporadically turn up in Irish towns to read their works to a
not-much-bigger audience has achieved recognition at 34.[5]

She described Hartnett's new home:

Here, four miles from the village, he is decamping from Raheny with
his wife and here for the next year at any rate, he will rear their two

children, grow potatoes and fatten piglets for curing (and pickling, 'I'm going to stretch that money as long as I possibly can'). Here too, he can find time to write in seclusion.[6]

Hartnett began preparations to leave Dublin and said goodbye to his colleagues in the telephone exchange with few regrets. In O'Neill's Pub in Trinity Street he held a celebration:

> That night they were all back at the switchboard for his final stint on the country exchange which he has worked for the past six years before taking his year's leave of absence. If you couldn't get Hackballscross 3 all evening, it was probably for reasons of poetic excess.[7]

Word also came through that he would receive a creative writing bursary from the Arts Council. The recognition and the financial support were gratifying. According to *The Irish Times*, on receipt of the bursary from the Arts Council, he was asked if he had anything to say: 'Michael Hartnett called on the finer flowers of both languages to say "*Táimse* flabbergasted"… It is possible that Michael was indicating gently that his transition towards his vow to write only in Irish in future is already taking place.'[8] Seamus Heaney and John B. Keane (among others) may have been instrumental in the Arts Council granting the bursary to Hartnett. Up to that time the policy of the Arts Council had been to give grants to organisations rather than individuals.[9]

Hartnett was glad to get out of the capital as he had grown disillusioned. His career, after such a bright beginning with the publication of his early poems in *Poetry Ireland* in 1962, had stagnated over the years. While he was still getting poems published regularly in the various literary magazines, the collections of his works had not made the impact he would have wishéd. Perhaps he felt it was time for a change. If there was a precedent for Hartnett's action it was that of renowned composer Seán Ó Riada fourteen years previously. Ó Riada, who had been born John Reidy, had given up living in Dublin in 1961 and moved to rural Cúil Aodha in Cork:

> Ó Riada's Dublin friends felt his life as a composer was finished when he left the city for Cúil Aodha in Autumn 1963, to take up his new post as a lecturer in the music department in University College Cork. They thought it bad enough that he should leave the capital city but to go to a small townland where he would have 'no intellectual stimulation such as he had enjoyed in Dublin appalled them. Where would he get the inspiration a composer needs? What was in store for him? Worse still, he had no telephone to link him with life in the big city and he didn't reply to letters.[10]

His attitude to Irish society and the language was similar to that of Hartnett. Indeed, Ó Riada's struggles with his music, which Hartnett admired greatly, echoed Hartnett's struggle with his poetry. Writing in 1977, he acknowledged what Ó Riada had achieved.

> Seán Ó Riada has been given a lot of credit lately for his influence on the revival and popularisation of Irish traditional music: no man deserved such credit more. And the revolution he started was not simply musical, it was a cultural one. People, especially the young, wanted to know where such great music came from and what kind of society it came from.[11]

Ó Riada had a similar disregard for Dublin-based critics and what he perceived as their Anglo-Irish sensibility. In an open letter to

Charles Acton of *The Irish Times* in 1971, just months before his sudden death, he outlined his views:

> There are in this small island two nations: the Irish (or Gaelic) nation, and the Pale. The Irish nation, tiny as it is at the moment, has a long, professional literary band musical tradition. The Pale, on the other hand, has a tradition of amateurishness … Three hundred years of this Pale amateurishness are, however, ultimately boring. It has about the same relevance for the Irish nation as would have a column about bee-keeping in a tricyclists' monthly journal. Nevertheless, I suppose we should, at least, be grateful for the existence of the Pale; it pays much of our taxes, and occasionally pats us on the head.[12]

As Gréagóir Ó Dúill, himself a poet in both languages, pointed out, many writers had used both Irish and English.

> Poets … deal in linguistic challenge. It is one source of that frisson of conflict which is essential to art. Poets have always walked along and across the border between languages and may use the border crossing of translation as a way to deal with a dry period. Liam O'Flaherty's poems and short stories in Irish, his native language, equal his larger work in English; Patrick Pearse worked success-fully in both languages; Denis Devlin moved imaginatively from French to Irish to English … in the eighteenth century, Eoghan Rua Ó Suilleabhain attempted to *plámás* his way out of the navy with a praise-poem in English for Admiral Rodney. More recently, Ó Riordain admitted the seductive charm of the larger language enfolding him, while Ó Direain found himself doggedly setting his teeth to burn the stump as he had burnt the candle, and to continue to develop his art in his native language. Behan wrote a few poems in Irish at about the time Beckett was shifting into French, but the bulk of his work was in English. MacLiammoir's

English birth and upbringing does not prevent his poetry in Irish being still enjoyed.[13]

However, none of these writers had made as expressly political a declaration as Hartnett. One writer who had headed down a similar route (though he came from an older generation) was Eoghan Ó Tuairisc (Eugene Watters) – like Hartnett and Ó Riada he had changed his name over the years. As somebody who had written in both languages, by 1975 Ó Tuairisc found himself in a similar position to Hartnett; a dilemma which he labelled 'psychic partition':

> The writer in modern Ireland is faced with the problem of the two cultures, the rich Gaelic culture with over a thousand years of literary endeavour in its texture, and the very rich but very different English culture which lies behind what has become the spoken speech over most of the island. It was easier for the English writer in Ireland fifty years ago – for those such as Yeats, Synge, Lady Gregory, Somerville and Ross, to whom the Gaelic culture was at most a rumour, half-heard in peasant speech and guessed at in translation. Since then a veritable revolution has been accomplished – mainly by the Gaelic League and the schools – and every English-speaking writer of this generation has a firsthand knowledge of the quality and content of the Gaelic tradition. He feels himself pulled both ways by the brilliant linguistic artistry of Chaucer, Shakespeare, Pope, Jane Austen, on the one hand, and on the other by the innate 'Irishry' and curious Celtic world-view of such magnificent artists as Aogán Ó Rathaille, Brian Merriman, Blind Raftery and the modern masters, Ó Cadhain, Ó Criomhthain, Ó Direain.[14]

This was the predicament that Ó Tuairisc/Watters faced:

Which is his tradition? The inescapable fact is that spiritually he belongs to both cultures. He suffers from a divided mind. If he writes in Irish he feels he has to close his mind and memory to many overtones and insights of the English incisiveness which the Irish language will not accommodate; if he writes in English he finds that medium which will not distil the earthy allusiveness and indefinable nuances of meaning which he has glimpsed in the Irish tradition. He experiences a cultural schizophrenia.[15]

Watters traced the political and social problems of the country back to this split:

It is not too much to say that the political partition of the island and the storm and stress of emotion it involves is but the external symbol of the inner dichotomy of the spirit experienced by every sensitive Irishman, North, South, East and West. After more than a score of years struggling with the problem, as a creative writer in both Irish and English, I can come up with no general solution … I outline my own personal experience merely, and my own attempt at a personal solution of the psychic partition.

Watters came up with his own solution with regard to the problem of writing in the two traditions. He used the English form of his name for his English writing, and the Irish form, Ó Tuairisc, for his Irish work; he had a dual identity, in literary terms at least. And over the years the interaction between the two languages developed. Ó Tuairisc outlined his shifting approach:

As a young man, in verse, fiction and drama, I took the view that both traditions had to be thoroughly mastered – Irish back into Old Irish times, English back to the Anglo-Saxon times of Caedmon and

the delightful *Exeter Book*, plus a thorough immersion in the contemporary spoken speech of both cultures. No easy matter, but one
was young and seriously engaged in exploring the human enigma
through the medium of words.[16]

Ó Tuairisc developed his literary split identity and maintained it
over the years, as he published material in both languages: poetry,
novels and plays, as well as essays and criticism:

> One was a dual personality –'Eoghan Ó Tuairisc' for Irish, 'Eugene
> Watters' for English. I was aware of course, that there was a good
> deal of carry-over, mostly unconscious in the hypnosis of composi-
> tion, from one language to the other. But still the dichotomy, the
> double face imposed an immense strain, and as the years went on
> it finally became unbearable. I had at length to make the decision:
> which was to be the dominant in my psychic genes? Which of the
> two personae ... was to be the living artist and which the spectre
> haunting the twilight of the imagination, and enriching the work
> from its own secret sources?

Ó Tuairisc felt that, over the years, the Irish side had grown
stronger as the English one weakened:

> For some time past, as reader and critic, I had become very uneasy
> in face of the degeneration of written English in Ireland. It seemed
> to me that much of the intellectual sinew had decayed from the lan-
> guage, much of the incisive verbal edge which had made it in the past
> such a fine instrument for the exploration of world experience. It
> had become flashy, flippant, flatulent, literatesque. I set this down to
> the decay of the Anglo-Irish cultural class in the democratization of
> society and imagined that 'the Great Tradition' of English might still
> be flourishing on its native soil. Then, last April, I was among those

chosen to represent Ireland at the Cambridge Poetry Festival. There I was appalled to find that the decay of English, the flatulence and the flippancy, was even more advanced that it was at home.[17]

He came to a decision like Hartnett's, the main difference being that he did not publicise it at the time:

> Rightly or wrongly I came to the conclusion that from now on I am an Irish writer writing in Irish, that Irish is a vital force in a devitalised society, that my fate is to spend the rest of my creative life as 'Eoghan Ó Tuairisc' blindly cultivating my own square mile of literary territory, bringing Irish idiom to bear on all aspects of life in town and country throughout Ireland, allowing the vibration of our English tradition to pass over as it may into the trickle of modern writing in Irish. It is a serious decision. It means poverty and obscurity and a constant struggle to make ends meet as a working artist without other source of income. Yet there is an immense relief of the spirit, a sense of homecoming.[18]

Like Hartnett, Ó Tuairisc had a strong, almost mystical belief in the power of language:

> There is a close association between dialect and a person's way of thinking. The person who changes his dialect changes his mind, his outlook on the world; because of this he may succeed in the outside world but he ties a tight fetter on his own personality; he damages the psyche inside, where the imagination is built on the speech of the environment from which it was shaped.[19]

Unlike many who saw Irish as a dead language, Ó Tuairisc saw it as a living organism, in written and in oral form:

But, again and again, it is renewed and revived from two sources: on one side from the Gaeltacht, from the firesides in the wilderness, from the city back streets and back rooms, from the farm, from the boat and from the parochial patois. And, on the other side, from the books and the manuscripts, from the old Irish sagas, from the myths, from the Annals, the historical tales, the theological and technical essays, and mostly and particularly from the songs and poems of the bards and poets who suffered hardship and poverty, exile, persecution and often enough even death – the bards and the poets who became travelling beggars from one bardic school to another seeking a precise knowledge of their trade, until they expended their lives and their health, forsook the everyday responsibilities and burned the midnight oil: 'Just to lie down for seven nights with pure Irish'. Learning his trade it is from these two sides, from the living language and from the poets, that a language is renewed.[20]

Ó Tuairisc was optimistic for the future:

In this little war that I'm waging I'm not worried about the living language but the written literature. And this is what I ask of the author – poet, newspaper prophet, or television wizard – that he should learn his trade, that he should go to the bardic schools, visiting the authorities, and at least, that he should learn the spelling, grammar, and syntax of the National Language. For myself, I haven't mastered the national spelling and grammar, but I'm learning … I'm no expert in these matters; my own art is enough for me, my life is too short for that art, and let the authorities decide on, and show us, a literary standard. I don't mind which standard …[21]

Of course, the other Irishman with many names was Brian O'Nolan/Brian Ó Nualláin/Flann O'Brien/Myles na gCopaleen, who was a dedicated Irish speaker but who also despised much of the language policy of official Ireland. O'Brien wrote a novel, *An*

Béal Bocht, satirising the rural miserableness of so many books in Gaelic. The book was set in the fictional Gaeltacht of Corcadora-gha, from which all the other Gaeltachts could be seen:

> the countryside of the Rosses and Gweedore, Bloody Foreland yonder and Tory Island far away out, swimming like a great ship where the sky dips into the sea. Looking out of the door, you could see the West of County Galway with a good portion of the rocks of Connemara, Aranmore in the ocean out from you with the small bright houses of Kilronan … From the window on the left you could see the Great Blaskets … and over yonder was Dingle with its houses close together … It singled out with particular venom the narrow, introverted, backward-looking bias, the shibboleths prevalent in sectors of the Irish culture language movement, the official lip-service paid to the Language Revival and the petrified mental attitudes associated with the establishment world of the Irish language. Mockery and insult, ridicule and sarcasm, parody and caricature were directed at these with a derisive bitterness that seemed at times close to total contemptuous rejection.[22]

As O'Brien put it, *An Béal Bocht* was 'an enormous jeer at the Gaelic morons here with their bicycle-clips and handball medals'. He wanted to move the language away from its 'potatoes and *poitín* image'.

Hartnett's interest in the language developed gradually. As he described it himself he:

> began to speak Gaelic to a number of friends, some poets, some 'native' speakers, some both. In 1970 my mind began to become enmeshed in a bilingual chaos – poems abruptly changing languages in mid-version, words from one tongue insinuating themselves into poems written in the other.[23]

Eventually 'my brain succumbed to the flood of Gaelic I was pouring on it and I found myself able to think and write whole poems in it, however bad'.[24]

Of great importance to Hartnett was the memory of his early childhood, in particular the influence on him of his Irish-speaking grandmother, Brigid Halpin. As he'd said before, 'It was not until her death in 1967 that I realised I had known a woman who embodied a thousand years of Gaelic history.' He believed that 'the very countryside breathes it out and even if the language did die out, its ghost would never be laid'.[25]

> I can never see a time when Irish becomes a 'dead' language. Latin, for instance did not really die: it became Spanish, French ... Ours is the first generation since the Famine that is not under pressure of the master-race kind ... We do not consider the speaking of Irish as a social drawback, as a stigma, as a sign of deep ignorance. We either speak it or wish to see it restored countrywide, or we treat it with apathy.[26]

With regard to the language, Hartnett claimed to be an optimist: 'I see the language, strengthening, broadening. Our poets, playwrights and novelists are in touch with world literature as their ancestors never were. Our people are no longer a harassed peasantry.' However, he saw one major drawback: 'Our government's attitude is hostile and apathetic by turns.'[27]

12

'TO KILL A LANGUAGE IS TO KILL A PEOPLE'

Having learned Irish at the home of his grandmother, Hartnett claimed it was only when he went to school that he became aware of the conflict between both languages. He believed that Irish as a language was endangered, because it was taught as a contrived, rule-laden entity, with little or none of the attraction that it held for him at home.

The economic improvement in the west in the 1970s had exacerbated the tendency of Gaelic-speaking and partly Gaelic-speaking districts to abandon Irish for English, which was 'the language of tourism and of the multinational corporations and foreign companies' that had located factories in those areas.[1]

As Gearóid Ó Tuathaigh put it in 1977:

> the difficulties of maintaining a 'national identity' have become greater since the foundation of the state, with the development in transport and communications, television and popular literature, all tending to reinforce the dominant Anglo-American cultural gulf-stream in which we are trapped.[2]

Hartnett felt that Irish society was losing something precious. The Irish language for the Irish people was the 'final sign that we are human/Therefore not a herd'. There was a political aspect to his views as he disliked the attitude of the coalition government of the time 'that Irish was an embarrassing language to have – you couldn't trade with it in Brussels':[3]

> Our government decided that the Franco-German policy of turning all Europe into a factory, with land and food supplies controlled by the state, was a good idea. So all things not conducive to trade were to be jettisoned, small shops, small farmers and, of course, Gaelic.[4]

In the *Irish Times* article explaining his decision to write in Irish, Hartnett repeated a story which he admitted might not even be true: 'it was alleged that a child had died in a Galway hospital asking for *deoch uisce* (a drink of water) and no one understood it'.[5] Variations on this 'hospital story' were a common theme in Gaelic circles at the time. As far back as 1966, an American student had told *The Irish Times*, 'you hear about Irish-speaking kids going to hospital and asking for something and not being understood'. [6]

In 1974, Hartnett was particularly concerned at the attitude of politicians to the Irish language. He specifically mentioned two reports in *The Irish Times* in February 1974 which had greatly agitated him and goaded him into taking the action he did.[7] Charles McCarthy of the Irish Association and Conor Cruise O'Brien, the Minister for Posts and Telegraphs in the Fine Gael–Labour coalition government had both spoken about the Republic's approach to the Irish language. A trade unionist and member of the RTÉ Authority, Charles McCarthy had addressed a meeting of the Irish Association on the topic of 'Education for a power-sharing society': 'With the prospect now of a political society spanning the whole island the dominance of the Gaelic sub-culture in the South and the tribalism in the North would become unsustainable'. McCarthy argued that in the south the political parties were not as polarised but the problem was no less tribal:

> The dominant sub-culture, the Gaelic Catholic sub-culture of the south has been, until recently so unassailable that it was quite unconscious of the basic injustice of its position. The fact is that it viewed other minority sub-cultures in the south as somehow alien.[8]

Hartnett saw these views as a veiled threat to the language, particularly as McCarthy was a member of the RTÉ Authority.

With the flare-up of the Troubles in Northern Ireland and the prospect, however remote, of unification, it was felt by McCarthy that the promotion of the Irish language in the Republic was a barrier to closer ties with Northern Ireland, and that state support for the language should be removed.

While this was worrying enough for Hartnett, Conor Cruise O'Brien spoke at the Jacobs' Awards ceremony where he announced his intention to amend the Broadcasting Authority Act – in particular, Section 17 – which required RTÉ to bear in mind the national aim of restoring and developing the national language:

> I have great respect for the Irish Language ('you better' came a heckle from the crowd) but very little respect for what is called 'the first official language'. The first official language and the narrow concept of the national culture go hand in dreary hand.
>
> The whole term 'national culture' needs to be examined. Nationality is an aspect of culture but not the whole of it. Is the language that I am speaking now, the language that most of us speak most of the time part of our national culture or is it not? If it is part of our culture then our culture is gratifyingly widespread on this planet. If it

is not part of our culture then our culture is unique since it does not include the language we actually speak.[9]

Speaking later to Dick Walsh of *The Irish Times*, O'Brien admitted that:

I did formulate it rather sharply. I hoped that I would make people sit up. Considering it afterwards, I thought that, yes, I had made people sit up and hurt some feelings unnecessarily, the feelings of those who were sincerely and strongly attached to certain things.[10]

Hartnett was one of the people offended, and was by no means the only one. O'Brien's biographer, D. H. Akenson, recounted how, on the night in question, O'Brien's wife (noted Gaelic writer Máire Mhac an tSaoi) took a phone call from Dónall Ó Móráin of Conradh na Gaeilge, and had to listen to him give out about her husband for over an hour. As O'Brien claimed ruefully:

I see signs that the diminution of compulsion and hypocrisy in this area are leading not to less but to more interest in the Irish language. My wife was inclined to doubt whether this would happen. I think she would now agree that, from her contacts, this would appear to be so.[11]

Hartnett became a member of Citizens for Better Broadcasting (CBB), an organisation created to foster informed attitudes and policies in the area of broadcasting. Its members included a wide cross-section of interests from the world of 'writing, theatre, sport, trade unionism and the churches': General Michael Costello, Father James McDyer, Tomás Mac Anna, Seán Ó Siocháin, Father Austin Flannery, Rev. Terence McCaughey, Bryan MacMahon and a cluster of academics, including Senator Augustine Martin, who was chairman of the organisation.[12]

The CBB accused the coalition government of 'shameful subservience to the cultural and political policies of the handful of states which dominate international mass communications'. The international flow of TV material was largely one-way, with the US and Britain between them exporting almost three times more material than the rest of the world combined. The CBB's main adversary was Conor Cruise O'Brien, in his role as minister with responsibility for broadcasting, particularly in regard to his policy towards the Irish language. O'Brien, writing after he was no longer a government minister, outlined his attitude to the language situation in Ireland:

> We have two official languages, the second is the one we use, the first is the one we think we ought to be using. We don't read – and most of us can't read – the writers who use the first official language, but we have some respect for them, in a vague and perfunctory sort of way … The Revival movement failed to revive, and its only movement was backwards. But it did generate a huge amount of political hypocrisy and – what was worse, because more insidious – a habit of listening to official nonsense, in an approving sort of way, as you might listen to the prattle of an innocent child. The Gaelic Revival failed to persuade the Irish people to speak Irish. But it did succeed in something. It succeeded in securing the lip-service of the great majority of the elected representatives of the Irish people (in this Republic). And it succeeded in making the Irish people a little ashamed of the fact that they continue to speak English and not Irish. The shame is not sufficient to bring about a resolve to learn Irish properly, and use it habitually. If it were sufficient to do that, that might be a very good thing. But it is sufficient to make us feel permanently ill at ease with the language we actually do speak … I

don't know whether there is any other people which habitually speaks one language, while feeling that it ought to be speaking another.[13]

As Minister for Posts and Telegraphs, O'Brien was in charge of RTÉ, and announced that he was going to introduce legislation to change its aims, in effect diluting its obligation to promote the Irish language.

Hartnett disagreed with any diminution of the state's commitment to Irish and resolved to do something about it. In a sense it was more for personal than for political reasons, his own tribute to his own particular heritage. Hartnett only wished that he could have better Irish. As Paul Durcan, who had been a close friend of Hartnett through the 1960s, saw it, 'Hartnett brooded on the question of race, language and landscape'.[14] He longed 'to belong to the ancient, rural Gaelic-speaking, aristocratic tribe but again and again he is betrayed and embarrassed by what he terms his "traitor larynx"'.[15] He did not want to align himself with the language revival movement of the 1970s: 'My main and most simple reason for changing to Gaelic is that I love the language (I have no interest in Conradhs, Cumanns, Comisiúns or churches).'[16]

Hartnett had little confidence in Ireland's ruling class:

Our hucksters are blind to anything but the making of a bob: our politicians (most of them) want only power, which is also money. One taste of Europe or the United Nations convinces them that Ireland and its problems are small beer indeed: their talents become too huge for our small stage and all the clowns want to play Hamlet … Our Europe-infatuated politicians are also like our Catholics after the Famine. The latter regarded Irish as a fetter which bound them to a devastated land, to a fourth-class citizenship: it was equated with illiteracy, poverty and mental deficiency. The politicians now consider Irish, at best as an antique, like the Ardagh chalice, fit only for the museum, redolent of a backward nation, a non-industrialised country, a direct pointer to the peasant background. It is an impediment to capitalism, they cannot sell it, they cannot trade in it.

He did not think that entry into the EEC had been good for the country:

In my view, the EEC's object is to secure the control of food supplies and their prices; that is the real way to rule. The symptoms of its partial success are small so far – beef mountains and expensive beef, milk surpluses and dear milk – no ducks, no duck-eggs, no farm eggs (only the concentration camp type); the phasing out of small farms and small farmers – the modern European equivalent of the Highland Clearances.[17]

However, he did hold out some hope for the future:

There is an air of pride about. The older people are beginning to regret the loss of the language. It wins prizes, it is spoken on radio and television. They are slowly beginning to disassociate it from the *duidín*, the *caipín* and the pig-in-the-parlour vision of themselves that their parents and their priests warned against. Prizes, etc., may be considered dubious carrots to hang before asses. But they work.[18]

Hartnett was not confident that his words would be heeded: 'It is always dangerous for a poet to dabble in politics or economics but it is safe for him to indulge in prophecy: nobody ever listens.' He had little time for politicians, or for those in power at any rate. As he told Desmond Rushe of the *Irish Independent*, he was making 'a gesture of contempt for all Irish governments since the Confederation of Kilkenny in 1642. All of them … deprived Gaelic of its rightful place.'[19]

To Hartnett, language was inextricably bound up with national identity. 'Language is the soul of its people, who for centuries have refined it and moulded it to express themselves.'[20] His gesture was in homage to his past. He felt that he 'knew Irish in his blood'. In a radio interview in 1975 he explained, 'All four of my grandparents were Gaelic-speakers. So my racial soul has only been English-speaking for eighty years, Gaelic-speaking for a thousand before it. The fabric is still in me. The marrowbone, the Gaelic marrowbone is still there.'[21]

As a poetic metaphor this may have been true, but literally it was not. As Hartnett knew, a language had to be learned. Pearse Hutchinson, perhaps the poet whose views were closest to those of Hartnett, dedicated a poem to Hartnett called 'The Frost is all over'. It begins with the statement, 'To kill a language is to kill a people', and ends with 'to kill a language is to kill one's self …'[22]

In the article that Hartnett wrote for *The Irish Times* explaining his decision to cease writing in English, he concluded:

> that any language would be allowed to die and that poets who are acquainted with it, borrow from it and even love it, should do nothing, is to me, incomprehensible. I only wish that I was better known and a better poet so that my decision was more remarkable and less unaccountable and 'amusing'.[23]

13

'THE CLINGING BLOOD UPON THE STONES'

Irish academic Declan Kiberd has expressed the opinion that 'the evidence suggests that Hartnett was keen to de-link the Irish language from narrow-gauge nationalism and especially from a nationalism that used Irish for its own purposes'.[1] However, Hartnett was not immune to being influenced by events in Northern Ireland as indeed many writers were at the time. In 1973, he had made some belligerent comments to a French journalist from *Les Lettres Nouvelles*, in an article entitled 'Ecrivains Irlandais'. Hartnett told Serge Fauchereau that:

> I believe in the gun, especially vis-à-vis Englishmen ... the presence of an English uniform on Irish soil is an insult to the Irish people ... I would be ready to fight. I do not understand everything that is going on in the North but I suffer on account of it ... I expect invasion ... I am ready. I know how to shoot, to hurl a grenade.[2]

Perhaps because it was published in a French journal his remarks created little stir in Ireland, though the ever vigilant John Jordan took notice in his column in *Hibernia*:

> Surely Mr Hartnett does not mean that the bulk of the million Loyalists in the North, who do accept British uniforms on Irish soil,

are not Irish? Surely he does not mean that he is in illegal possession of guns and grenades? And would he make comparable statements in English in, for instance, *The Irish Times*?[3]

The worsening situation in Northern Ireland may have influenced Hartnett at the time. Even as placid a character as Tyrone-born John Montague was called to task by John Jordan for remarks he had made in the same issue of *Les Lettres Nouvelles*; that in Northern Ireland at the time violence was 'necessary'.

One cannot dispute that Hartnett held strong nationalist views at that time. In 1971, in a review in *The Irish Press* of a poetry collection called *The Young British Poets*, he took grave offence at some of the choices:

> The inclusion here of Derek Mahon, Michael Longley, and Seamus Heaney, I find disturbing. Politically speaking I suppose, a person living in Belfast can be described both as British and Irish and can take advantage of this when the opportunity arises. Spiritually speaking however, there can be no hedging: poets belong to their own countries; no arbitrary borders should confuse them. ... I believe that at the present time there should be no room for ambiguity: poets from the Six Counties should specifically declare themselves for one side or the other.[4]

In his poem 'A Visit to Castletown House' (which became part of the *Farewell to English* collection in 1975, but had actually been published in *The Irish Press* in April 1971), Hartnett described his feelings on attending a classical recital at such a remnant of British rule in Ireland. Castletown House, the largest Palladian-style house in Ireland, had been built in 1722, for the then Speaker of the Irish House of Commons, William Conolly. It had remained in the possession of the Conolly family until 1965. While he liked the music and appreciated the architecture of the house and its setting in the landscape, Hartnett could not help thinking of the colonial oppression and exploitation that had made such beauty possible:

> I went into the calmer, gentler hall
> in the wineglassed, chattering interval:
> there was the smell of rose and wood smoke there.
> I stepped into the gentler evening air
> and saw black figures dancing on the lawn,
> Eviction, Droit de Seigneur, Broken bones,
> and heard the crack of ligaments being torn
> and smelled the clinging blood upon the stones.[5]

For Hartnett, the concept of an 'Irish soul' was wrapped up in the idea of a Gaelic-speaking people. The two were inseparable. Many writers in Ireland tussled with the problem of a 'divided mind', to use Thomas Kinsella's label for the dilemma facing them. In an influential Thomas Davis lecture Kinsella stated:

> The two languages and their poetry may never have had much to do with each other – may even at times have been unaware of each other's existence; and certainly our poetry in English has never been isolated from English poetry, much to the benefit of poetry in general. But the separation between the two languages was never complete, and neither was the connection between the two literatures. If we realise this we may become aware of a vital reality – one that has everything to do with the 'divided mind' of the modern Irish poet …[6]

It was not a problem English poets faced:

A modern English poet can reasonably feel at home in the long tradition of English poetry. No matter what his preoccupations may be, he will find his forebears there, and he apparently feels free to conscript an Irish or an American poet into the tradition if that seems necessary ... An Irish poet has access to all of this through his use of the English language, but he is unlikely to feel at home in it ...

Kinsella felt that he had to go back to the 1700s to discover any worthwhile poetry:

I believe that silence, on the whole, is the real condition of Irish literature in the nineteenth century – certainly of poetry ... yet to come on eighteenth-century Irish poets after the dullness of the nineteenth century is to find a world suddenly full of life and voices, the voices of poets who expect to be heard and understood and memorised ... they are at home in their language and tradition ... beyond them again is Aogán Ó Rathaille, the last major poet in Irish and beyond him the course of Irish poetry stretching back more than a thousand years, full of riches and variety. In all of this I recognise a great inheritance and, simultaneously, a great loss ... I recognise that I stand on one side of a great rift, and can feel the discontinuity in myself. It is a matter of people and places as well as writing – of coming from a broken and uprooted family, of being drawn to those who share my origins and finding that we cannot share our lives.[7]

Hartnett knew which side of the 'great rift' he stood on. Influenced as they were by events in Northern Ireland, his convictions may not have been constant. On the death of the hunger striker Bobby Sands in 1981 he wrote a poem that was regarded at the time as too inflammatory to be published in *The Irish Times*, but it was later included in *A Book of Strays*. The poem 'Who killed Bobby Sands?' was based on 'Who killed Cock Robin?' (and may also have echoed Patrick Kavanagh's 'Who killed James Joyce?' which also used the question-and-answer format of the nursery rhyme):

'Who caught his blood?'
'I,' said a Provo,
'with my little black hood,
I caught his blood.'

'Who'll carry his coffin?'
'We,' said the terrorists,
shaking hands and scoffing,
'we'll carry his coffin.'

The poem concluded:

All the children of Ireland
wrung their little hands
when they heard of the death
of poor Bobby Sands.[8]

In 1985, in a review of the work of Desmond Egan, Hartnett looked back ruefully at the problems writers felt:

As in the case of all Irish poets working since the 1970s the baleful subject of Northern Ireland has bruised him. The tide of this fashionable tragedy has washed ashore many mediocre poets and writers who treat it simply as copy.[9]

He recalled:

A couple of years ago I shared a radio programme with Dr Noel Browne. We talked about the poet's position in society. I believed then, and still believe, that the poet should steer clear of political issues. Dr Browne did not agree. I said I could not write about the north, because I had never been there and was not involved, though the deaths and maimings there angered and sickened me. To relieve these feelings, of course, I could write privately.

Hartnett did not feel that he should publish such poems. However, in the *Farewell to English* collection one of the poems dealt with the politics of a country that Hartnett had only visited on a couple of occasions, when he had been the recipient of a grant from the Irish–American Cultural Institute to go on lecture tours. The poem 'USA' contained some harsh language and imagery:

> They chained the land and pulled her down
> and nailed her to the sea with towns.
> She lies on her back, her belly cut in fields
> of red and yellow earth. She does not yield,
> she is not theirs. She does not love this race.
> She will not open her legs to enclose
> the scum of Europe, jockeying for grace.[10]

Some years later, Dennis O'Driscoll asked Hartnett about his attitude to the United States with particular reference to the poem.

Q. The poem, 'USA', has always surprised me by its vituperation. It refers to the inhabitants of that country as 'the scum of Europe', whereas many Irish would think of it as the place where their more unfortunate relatives were forced to emigrate.

A. I was always treated well on my visits to the States. But I was taken to an Indian reservation in Minnesota and to various burial grounds. I felt the incredible lack of the Indian nation and the total lack of knowledge of the Indians on the part of the people who were living on their lands. Europeans of whatever origin are tarred with the same brush in the poem. When I see soft-centred American T.V. programmes about these brave people going out to cultivate their lands and grow pumpkins, I get annoyed.[11]

When his decision to give up writing in English became widely known in literary circles, Hartnett awaited the reaction. He had always had a wary attitude to critics and, as he told Dennis O'Driscoll, he was content 'to be a small fish in a small pond, though this particular pond happens to be full of piranhas'.[12] As Allan Gregory put it, 'critical response to Hartnett had been generally favourable with many seeing him as the great white hope of Irish poetry'.[13]

At the time, Hartnett was moving restlessly between publishers. No longer with New Writers' Press, he was contracted to have books published by both The Gallery Press and Goldsmith Press in 1975. The Gallery Press was run by Peter Fallon, a poet himself, and had started up in 1970. As Fallon explained:

It wasn't started with a mission or manifesto; it did evolve out of an energy I felt, and out of an absence. In the late 1960s there were magazines and readings, the energy of youth. I was doing readings with some friends who were starting to write, and out of all this came a small magazine, *Capella*.[14]

Fallon was involved with a group called *Tara Telephone*, which also featured another young poet and man-about-town, Eamon Carr. Fallon and Carr published the occasional magazine called

Capella, which was distinguished by a Jim Fitzpatrick cover showing Celtic heroes. Eamon Carr was the drummer with Irish rock group *Horslips*. Fallon became increasingly interested in publishing. 'The first books appeared between issues of the magazine, almost supplements.'[15] Fallon, who was from Meath, based his publishing company there. Unlike Dolmen and New Writers' Press, Gallery did not do their own printing. It was purely a publishing venture.

Hugh McFadden of *The Irish Press* attended a poetry reading in the Player's Theatre at Trinity College in March 1975 (before *A Farewell to English* was actually published). Hartnett read poems in both Irish and English, and it was so well attended that Peter Fallon had to draw back the red velvet curtains of the stage so that the overflow audience could see the poet. Before reading the poem 'A Farewell to English' he 'talked around the reasons' why he was abandoning writing in that language.

At the reading, McFadden felt that Hartnett had an apprehensive attitude to his declaration, as if he was expecting disapproval. 'Guardedly, he prefaced the reading by commenting that it was written for those that were interested.'[16] He had by this stage composed one long poem in Irish – 'Cúlú Íde' ('The Retreat of Ita Cagney') – and, at readings, would switch from English to Irish halfway through. McFadden described Hartnett's reading of 'Cúlú Íde' as a memorable and disturbing moment. 'When he ended, the respectful silence was broken in relief. It is impossible to say how much of the meaning was lost – I must admit that I understood only the intention.'[17]

Another reading did not go so well, and it was Hartnett's use of the Irish language that caused disquiet:

The decision had been broadcast in the readings and interviews that prefaced the appearance of *A Farewell to English*. I remember attending one such reading. It must have taxed the politeness of those who had come expecting poetry spoken in the only language they understand – English – and were made instead to shuffle nervously in their seats while the poet recited passage after passage from his 'Cúlú Íde'. The applause when it came, was decorous and ignorant – par for the course in some respects – except that on this occasion it concealed deeper feelings; of embarrassment perhaps, or anger. Hartnett's utterance of a Gaelic poem in such surroundings was a deliberate provocation of his audience, implying as it did that his incomprehensibility was their fault ... By abandoning one language for another in the middle of a reading, Hartnett had rendered not merely the development of his devotion to Gaelic, he had effectively dramatised the consequences of his commitment. Most of his audience could no longer understand him.[18]

Goldsmith Press published a dual language version of *The Retreat of Ita Cagney/Cúlú Íde* as part of Hartnett's transition to writing purely in Irish, and the Irish version was printed in an Old Gaelic script for added effect. As the blurb went:

> *The Retreat of Ita Cagney/Cúlú Íde* marks a turning point in Michael Hartnett's poetic development. Having consolidated his position as one of the most contemporary Irish poets writing in English ... Hartnett has now decided to write and publish in Irish only. In this book then, we have both the last of his English and the first of his Irish poems. The two versions are related – variations, it might be said, on the same theme ... Should he have turned his back on English? Should he have switched over completely to Irish? Can it be done? Such questions will not be decided by argument, but by the quality of Hartnett's writing in Irish.[19]

Many critics took the opportunity to compare Hartnett's proficiency in both languages. Douglas Sealy in his review was of the opinion that 'he has not yet got the facility and skill in Irish that he has in English'.[20] John Jordan was more positive about the poem, which was 'a small-town mini-epic, so redolent of Hardy'.[21]

In an interview in March 1975, Elgy Gillespie asked Hartnett what was the reaction of his friends to his announcement that he would no longer write in English:

'Oh, amusement.'

'No concern that you might be doing yourself out of new admirers and shrinking a fond audience?'

'Listen, it's impossible to limit my audience, it's so small already.'[22]

14

'A LONG WAY TO COME FOR NOTHING'

A Farewell to English was published in 1975 by The Gallery Press. Hartnett dedicated the titular poem to Brendan Kennelly.

Irish poet, Augustus Young expressed a certain cynicism about Hartnett's decision. He said that Hartnett's:

> is a strong dislocated voice. Though the power has yet to come. His highly developed sense of craft is more in the Gaelic tradition than the Anglo-Irish. He is said to be reverting to Gaelic (virtually a dead language). This would be a pity as it isn't his first language, and he uses English superbly. However, thems [*sic*] who write in Gaelic get the grants … His experiment, writing in an adopted language, might prove more interesting than I give him credit. An awful lot of second-raters have tried it and failed … Hartnett is first-rate and dedicated.[1]

Hartnett explained the background to *A Farewell to English* to Elgy Gillespie of *The Irish Times*:

> I decided to burn my bridges with that poem. Obviously the thing needs some qualifications made. I can't stop myself from writing in English. At the moment I am writing spontaneously in both languages but I will never publish English poems in Ireland again.

The journalist added, 'at this point, and I don't think he'll mind me saying so, he looks slightly uncomfortable'.[2]

A Farewell to English had two launches, the first in June 1975, at Trinity College as part of a Gallery Press package with works by Brendan Kennelly and Robert Greacen, and another at Listowel Writers' Week in October. The Trinity event was well attended: 'the hall packed on a sultry June night, a sense of poetry surviving the sun', according to *The Irish Times*. Hartnett was well received. The reviews were another story as it created less than a ripple. In literary circles the reaction, in public at least, was positive if muted, with one notable exception. By far the most scathing response came from Ciaran Carson in *The Honest Ulsterman*: 'I have admired Michael Hartnett's work for some time and it gives me no pleasure to see him saying cheerio to the Saxon in such a half-assed way.'[3]

Carson was himself a poet and traditional musician. He was also an accomplished Irish speaker so his verdict was all the more devastating: '*A Farewell to English* is an unhappy book. It is by turns confused, derivative, lyrical, posturing and, on occasion, exact.'[4] It seemed that there was little in Hartnett's work that appealed to him: 'There are echoes here of Kinsella, bad Yeats, worse Kennelly'.[5] For Carson, the bad outweighed the good: 'Faced with the acreage of crap in the book, well-written lines tend to fade into sylph-like obscurity … The title poem itself is a hotch-potch of fierce hard writing …'[6]

Carson did not seem to think that Hartnett's action helped the cause of the Irish language. He claimed that:

I am sympathetic to anyone who feels that his own cause or the cause of a 'people' might be improved by writing in one language rather than another. Possibly self-publicisation might well help the cause, but in this case, any news seems to be bad news, and the whole affair has almost degenerated to the level of a real-life *Béal Bocht*.[7]

The same issue of *The Honest Ulsterman* contained an almost equally damning review by Carson of Seamus Heaney's *North*.

To show what a small and incestuous world it was in Irish poetry circles, Hartnett had given Heaney's *North* a very positive review in *The Irish Times*. The review also showed Hartnett's attitude to the literary circles in which he moved:

> There is no doubt about it, Seamus Heaney is a superb poet. Given the reservations of Dublin cliques – I heard one eminent 'critic' call him 'an emigrant', given the meanness of the minds of those in Ireland, North and South, who call themselves poets, whose spite and envy wouldn't have given the 'Good Thief' a chance – given my own expectancy, restlessness and insistence that a poet must move on, he has maintained his standard through three collections and surpassed them in *North*.[8]

Heaney was so pleased with the review he wrote to Hartnett to thank him.

As to Hartnett's *Farewell*, it perhaps did not create as strong an impact as he had hoped. Eiléan Ní Chuilleanáin gave it a guarded welcome:

> The farewell to English is not all there is to Michael Hartnett's collection of that name, although it is the aspect that has attracted public comment. At first sight the book even looks a bit disjointed, the early poems containing no reference to the language issue ... at the back of it all there's a single theme; violence and the responses to it ... When Hartnett faces the problems of the whole of Irish culture he's in a bit of trouble ... the persona is satiric but the satire is on a

narrow front … Much of it is satiric but not original; some, especially the first two sections, is personal and very good.[9]

Owing to the amount of publicity generated by Hartnett before publication, the collection could be seen as having to justify his decision. As David Collins pointed out:

The poems that comprise the collection may be read as a series of events not unlike the rumours, readings and statements that both preceded and coincided with their publication … This raises the question of the relation between poetry and propaganda.[10]

He felt that the poems could not be judged solely on their own terms:

Critical procedures that treat the poem as a self-enclosed and self-sustaining entity are inappropriate here. The poems simply refuse to be placed in that hygienic context, or to accommodate themselves to that disinterested, detached contemplation that is the pivot of the academic method. For these poems are didactic, they are intended to have a public consequence – hence their rhetorical idiom … The politics of the collection is inseparable from its linguistic attitudes … Yet it is the preoccupation with language which offers the collection an overall unity of expression which transcends the content of the individual poems.[11]

As Paul Durcan described it, the title poem is 'a personal testament of 167 lines of polemic, satire, nostalgia, indignation, prophecy and faith'.[12] In it Hartnett gave the background to his farewell:

I sunk my hands into tradition
sifting the centuries for words …

> … and I was flung back
> on the gravel of Anglo-Saxon …

> What was I doing with these foreign words?
> I, the polisher of the complex clause,
> wizard of grasses and warlock of birds,
> midnight-oiled in the metric laws?[13]

The poet meets old men on the summer road:

> They stopped before me with a knowing look
> hungry, snotnosed, half-drunk …

> They looked back once,
> black moons of misery
> sickling their eye-sockets,
> a thousand years of history
> in their pockets.[14]

In Part 3 the poet pictures W. B. Yeats as a cook:

> Chef Yeats, that master of the use of herbs
> could raise mere stew to a glorious height,
> pinch of saga, soupcon of philosophy
> carefully stirred in to get the flavour right,
> and cook a poem around the basic verbs.
> … sniff and stand back and proudly offer you
> the celebrated Anglo-Irish stew.[15]

Like many an Irish poet, Hartnett felt that W. B. Yeats had been an overwhelming influence and not always for the better. As he put it in *The Irish Times* in 1971: 'In an age when literary genius abounds talents that would otherwise shine are eclipsed and when that age produces such a triad as O'Casey, Synge and Yeats, minor poets and minor dramatists are counted minor indeed.'[16] He was particularly critical of Yeats' influence on certain Irish poets:

> … to our bugbear Mr Yeats/who forced us into exile/on islands of bad verse … Yeats, like Joyce, cast a suffocating shadow over literary Ireland: his work initiated a spate of plagiarism and poetic apathy which still survives in its last drab phrases among elderly men who are now in the main content to reminisce about Yeats himself and to produce the occasional piece of Celtic Twilightery.[17]

Hartnett had some sympathy for the writers who came after Yeats:

> It was the misfortune of these poets to be in the shadow of Yeats: if one of them chose to write on distinctly Irish themes he was immediately dubbed 'Celtic Twilight', and if he chose a more personal note he was dismissed.[18]

He disapproved of the way Yeats used Irish folklore and mythology:

> Whatever Yeats knew about other systems, Eastern or Western, whatever he knew about the English tradition, he knew very little about Ireland or the Irish tradition. He began by drawing on the fairy-tales and pishoguery of the west of Ireland: searching for the springs, he jumped right back to the Red Branch and Fenian Cycles and early legends and then leaped forward to Mangan, Davis and the Young Irelanders. It was as if, making England the breeding ground for his revival, he took Beowulf and Rossetti, assumed that there was nothing in between, and held this abortion up to the world as the English literary tradition and proceeded to develop it.

'Gaelic is my national language but it is not my mother tongue,'

Yeats had said. Hartnett was of the opinion that Yeats had constructed a false background, elevating such nineteenth-century poets as James Clarence Mangan, Thomas Davis and Samuel Ferguson to undeserved heights simply because they wrote in English:

> Yeats, desperately looking for a nation, included Mangan among his literary ancestors simply because there were very few to choose from who had written English verse in this country. That Yeats ignored 1,000 years of Gaelic verse and chose 'Davis, Mangan, Ferguson' as his poetic fathers is a typical Yeatsian bluff. He had flirted with Gaelic, could not master it and when he came to build his spiritual mansion he simply ignored it.[19]

In a discussion with Eavan Boland, Seamus Heaney and Liam Miller, Hartnett described his account of Yeats' working methods: 'I think Yeats believed, in part … if you scatter a few domestic animals like goats and cows and a few mythological heroes like Cuchulainn, you are creating an Irish literature.'[20] At the same time Hartnett appreciated the genius of Yeats. He advised all the young poets in Ireland to read up on Yeats:

> especially those who, through laziness or fear of their inability to produce a poem anywhere near as good as one of Yeats' will not read his biographies or collected poems or any study, for fear scholarship should blunt their natural talent for opacity.[21]

In Part 4 of 'A Farewell to English' the poet railed against the new Ireland:

> We knew we had been robbed
> but were not sure that we lost

the right to have a language
or the right to be the boss.
So we queued up at the Castle
in nineteen-twenty-two
to make our Gaelic
or our Irish dream come true.
We could have had from that start
made certain of our fate
but we chose to learn the noble art
of writing forms in triplicate …
We entered the Irish paradise
of files and paper-clips.[22]

In Part 5 he made his defiant farewell to English:

Poets with progress
make no peace or pact:
The act of poetry
is a rebel act.[23]

Aside from the outburst of alliteration, Hartnett seemed to be taking a conservative if not a reactionary stance, aligning himself and, by implication the Irish language, as backward-looking:

Gaelic is the conscience of our leaders,
The memory of a mother-rape they will
Not face, the heap of bloody rags they see
And scream at in their boardrooms of mock oak …
For Gaelic is our final sign that
we are human, therefore not a herd.[24]

The poem ends with a further affirmation of Hartnett's intention:

But I will not see
Great men go down
Who walked in rags
From town to town
Finding English a necessary sin
The perfect language to sell pigs in.

I have made my choice
and leave with little weeping:
I have come with meagre voice
To court the language of my people.[25]

The intensely personal nature of his poem was emphasised by 'my'. He had come to court the language of 'my people' just as he had referred to 'my Lorca holding out his arms'. In many ways perhaps the poem should have been called '*My* Farewell to English'.

Two poems in the collection referred to his Irish-speaking grandmother Brigid Halpin:

Ignorant in the sense
She ate monotonous food
And thought the world was flat,
And pagan, in the sense
She knew the things that moved
At night were neither dogs nor cats
But púcas and dark-faced men.[26]

'Death of an Irishwoman' ended with a list:

She was a summer dance at the crossroads.

> She was a card game where a nose was broken.
> She was a song that nobody sings.
> She was a house ransacked by soldiers.
> She was a language seldom spoken.[27]

In 'Mrs Halpin and the Lightning' Hartnett described his grandmother's superstitious ways and pagan beliefs:

> Her fear was not the simple fear of one
> who does not know the source of thunder:
> these were the ancient Irish gods
> she had deserted for the sake of Christ.[28]

'A Visit to Castletown House' was in form and content quite Yeatsian, or as Ciaran Carson put it 'there was a touch of the Willies' about it, which, given Hartnett's criticism of Yeats elsewhere in the collection, was a conscious irony.

In 'A Visit to Croom, 1745' he imagined a nightmarish journey at a time when Gaelic society was in severe decline, the people defeated. The conquered people's language was still Gaelic but the language of their rulers was English. Croom was where Hartnett had been born, a fact of which he was intensely proud. As he told Dennis O'Driscoll:

> I am the only 'recognised' living poet who was born in Croom, Co. Limerick, which was the seat of one of the last courts of poetry in Munster: Seán Ó Tuama and Andrias MacCraith. When I was quite young, I became very conscious of these poets and, so, read them very closely indeed. Through them, without going into their elaborate syntax, I became unafraid of rhetoric as such. I have been to hundreds of poetry readings and I have seen 'the best minds of

my generation' ruining their own poems because they are such bad readers. I believe, in an old Irish fashion, that you must be able to deliver the goods, stand up and give it out. So I am pro-rhetoric, but not fustian or bombast or anything like that.[29]

In 'A Visit to Croom, 1745', Hartnett outlined a dream vision:

I had walked a long time
in the mud to hear
an avalanche of turf fall down,
fourteen miles in straw-roped overcoat
passing for Irish all along the road
now to hear a Gaelic court
talk broken English to an English king.
It was a long way
to come for nothing.[30]

Another thread that ran through the collection was the urban-rural disparity. Other poems in the collection dealt with country customs and occasions: a pig-killing, a wake, a horse catcher. These rural activities were contrasted sharply with descriptions of an urban existence, reflecting that other big change in Hartnett's life; his move to Templeglantine. Some of the poems seemed to have no connection with one another, they were simply new poems that had not previously been issued in book form. Given the publicity generated by Hartnett before publication of the collection it might have been better if Gallery had published a more focused set of poems, with 'A Farewell to English' on its own or as part of a sequence that dealt solely with the language issue. This was, in many ways, why Ciaran Carson, perhaps the most trenchant public critic of Hartnett's *Farewell*, called it 'half-assed'. It could be argued that the variety of poems in the collection displayed the range of the poet's gifts and established and broadened the cultural context and sweep of the title poem. Or perhaps Hartnett himself was solely interested in getting the last of his poetry in English into print in book form thereby clearing the decks for his future writings in the Irish language.

Even before he left Dublin Hartnett had backtracked some-what on his original announcement. He told Elgy Gillespie of *The Irish Times* that he might write poems in English, he just wouldn't have them published. He made a similar point to Desmond Rushe of the *Irish Independent* when he told him that he would:

> not abandon English entirely, if the proper mode of expression for a poem is English, he will write it in that language but he is determined that only his Gaelic poetry will be published in this country in the future.[31]

Ciaran Carson in *The Honest Ulsterman* highlighted this very point.

> One wonders at the purpose of the whole book. Michael Hartnett is quoted that he wasn't really going to stop actually writing English, never mind talking it, he was going to stop publishing English poems. At least he thought so. Now, had he called his book *A Farewell to Published Poems written in the English Language* that might have been more honest, though no more explanatory of what exactly he is getting at.[32]

Seamus Heaney pointed out a similar-seeming contradiction, if in a less critical manner.

> *A Farewell to English* abounded in the paradoxes of the creative life. Its author was setting out to kill the thing he loved or rather love-

hated, and yet at that moment he was giving thrilling proof of how vividly the thing lived within him.[33]

Eamon Grennan was sympathetic to Hartnett's efforts and of the opinion that in the *Farewell to English* collection 'there is a keen plainness to such language as if the poet had clustered the self-regarding melodrama of his rhetoric but kept its kernel of intensity'.[34] However, he felt that as a whole, '"A Farewell to English" itself is an uneven poem with some sub-Kavanagh satire, a few clumsy swipes at Yeats and myopic, exclusive, pseudo-mystical claims for the Irish language.'[35] He disliked its 'rhetorical shrillness' and believed that Hartnett's 'abandonment of English … is our loss and, for the life of me, I cannot be sure whose gain'.[36]

Douglas Sealy in his *Irish Times* review was more sympathetic: 'Mr Hartnett's aim seems to be to get his feelings straight onto paper with an awkward sincerity which would be spoiled by paying too much attention to shaping the final product'.[37] John Jordan was of a similar view about his old protégé: 'he has established himself as a poet of starkness, not always of language, but always of feeling …'[38] Philip Marcus in *The Irish Press* felt:

> there is real emotion in *A Farewell to English*, emotion which the reader as well as the author can feel. And the scale here is the grand scale … The Yeatsian solution, an Irish literature in English, no longer seems viable … Even in dramatising the problem Mr Hartnett has made at least one permanent contribution to the tradition he feels he must renounce.[39]

Gabriel Rosenstock in the *Irish Independent* was generally supportive of Hartnett:

> We cannot fail to be impressed by his rebellious individualism, his

> refusal to be subservient to any false high-mindedness expected of poets
> … Hartnett … is often beset by complex poses and strained devices …
> but he is always at his best when unaffected and unambiguous.

Rosenstock was hopeful for Hartnett's development: 'If he avoids
the pitfalls of verbal academicals and gives rein to this thoroughly
engaging eloquence from the heart we can expect a golden harvest
when he comes to publish his future poems in Irish.' However,
he also felt many critics were not taking Hartnett seriously:
'The saddest part of it all is that the Anglo-Irish literati seem to
view Hartnett's rebellion with little more than faintly perplexed
amusement.'[40]

Not all Gaelic poets at the time were happy with Hartnett's
stance. Liam Ó Muirithile felt that in some way Hartnett was seen
by some people as 'more Gaelic' than the existing poets because of
what he had done. Though this was hardly Hartnett's intention,
it could not fail to cause resentment, this 'more Gaelic than thou'
attitude.[41]

However, there was still a major obstacle for the future. As
Hartnett told *The Kerryman* newspaper at the time, in a short
interview on the occasion of his relocation to Templeglantine, the
changeover from English to Irish had not been the easiest.

> It is extremely difficult but I am working very hard on it. I am read-
> ing as much as I can, especially the Irish poets but I am finding it
> difficult to produce good poetry. I'd say it will take me two or three
> years to sort myself out.[42]

Time would tell if he was being optimistic. Characteristically,
Hartnett told the paper that he was also working on a play.

15

'NO TOTEMS, NO GODS'

Back in Templeglantine it was evident that Hartnett had taken to the rural life with gusto as a radio documentary from the time recorded. "'I'll kill you in September," the poet exclaimed, to his bonham, the future source of black puddings, pork-steak, bacon and ham. The pig's name was Peter. "I'm going to salt Peter in September, you see."'[1] In a television clip from the time Hartnett's young son Niall is seen wrestling with the pig while his amused father looks on.[2]

Hartnett enjoyed the idea of being able to provide for his family by his own efforts: 'I love rabbits, I love to eat them, so I'll probably shoot them,' he admitted, adding that he was 'culinary-minded' about most of God's creatures.[3]

The household had three pets:

> … a cat with the earthy name of 'Black Bum', a Kilkenny hen by the name of 'Mrs Slim' who has lain an egg a day since February and 'Chief' the dog.

Now that he was safely away from his job as a telephonist he was willing to describe his seven years there as 'Hell'.[4] Rosemary Hartnett recalls:

> Michael was very happy to be living in West Limerick and away from the Dublin scene. He immersed himself in country lore and

poetry, and in the pub would chat away for hours with the locals in Newcastle West. However nobody around us spoke Irish and they regarded us as something of a novelty, whilst at the same time being friendly and welcoming. So he spent hours studying Irish and writing at home ...[5]

Nell McCafferty encountered him in Newcastle West, in July 1977, at one of Ireland's ubiquitous summer festivals, this one featuring the 'Lady of Desmond' beauty contest:

> ... the 31 young women sat shivering in bright dresses on the platform as the townspeople gawked at them ... One female with a mahogany tan drew much attention ... A magician was called to take the stage. 'He had been booked for a nightly appearance. He did not turn up. There's magic for you.'

However, as his friend and fellow writer Gabriel Fitzmaurice described it, 'unlike Joyce and the rest he didn't need to flee Ireland to be an exile'.[6] Fitzmaurice felt that Hartnett's stay in Templeglantine, though not much more than ten miles from where he was brought up, was an act of deliberate isolation. David Wheatley also saw Hartnett's relocation as a form of withdrawal:

> With the poets of Northern Ireland in the ascendant and those from the Republic almost disappearing in their shadow, outside Ireland at least, Hartnett chose to retreat to a Hidden Ireland both literal and metaphorical, moving from Dublin to West Limerick.[7]

Hartnett may have withdrawn from Dublin but he was determined to get involved with the community to which he had moved, so became an active member of the Labour Party.

He joined his father and his brother in the Newcastle West branch and, during the 1977 general election campaign, he was the Director of Elections for the Limerick West constituency. As he admitted wryly, he learned more about politics and politicians in the two weeks leading up to the vote on 16 June than he had ever known before. He admitted that he lost half a stone and his candidate lost his deposit.[8] In fact, the Labour Party candidate, County Councillor Ned Dwyer from Newcastle West, received 1,444 first preference votes. Hartnett saw no contradiction in actively supporting the party, despite opposing the policies of the coalition government of which it had been part. Conor Cruise O'Brien, whose attitude to the Irish language he had deplored, was a fellow member of the Labour Party.

Hartnett had a memorable encounter with an eminent politician in 1977. As *The Irish Press* reported:

> There was a 'happening' midway on the main road between Limerick and Killarney yesterday, and the passer-by may have been puzzled at the Tricolour floating lazily in the late May sun, a bonfire burning and the sound of bodhráns and traditional music rising over the sloping fields of West Limerick.[9]

President Patrick Hillery came to the 'parish of Templeglantine, with its nine townlands to present the Glor na nGael national … award. During 1975–76 Templeglantine was the area which did the most to promote the use of Irish in community life.' Hillery arrived in the early afternoon to be met by a piper and twenty bodhrán players dressed in green cloaks and gold caps, as they beat out 'The Rising of the Moon'. As the *Press* put it, 'the contented cows grazed away … as the farming folk celebrated'. The bodhrán was Templeglantine's symbol, and Dr Hillery was presented with one. Before he left he insisted on a lesson. A poem of welcome was composed specially in Irish by Michael Hartnett. In his 'Dán Fáilte', the poet invited the President to 'listen to the voice of Irish and you will get strength'.[10]

Hartnett, in his early years back in Templeglantine, acted as radio critic for *Hibernia*. Now that he no longer had a full-time job he had time to listen to the radio during the day. As he said himself, there he was with his Japanese transistor: 'Imagine me now, eight hundred and twenty feet above sea level ... and I tune in on the FM band and I pick up Gaelic voices from the three corners of Ireland.'[11] He used his radio column to discuss his various likes and dislikes with regard to the Irish version of country and western, the lack of comedy programmes on RTÉ and many other hobby horses. For a radio critic in Ireland Hartnett had one large drawback – his dislike of the country's leading broadcaster at the time, Gay Byrne, which he expressed in a somewhat tongue-in-cheek manner.

> I can't stand Gay Byrne ... His voice grates on my nerves. And yet I listen to his programme every morning and I watch his show every Saturday night. He is the supreme professional. RTÉ would be poor indeed without him.[12]

Hartnett admitted that some of it might be envy as so many of Gay Byrne's fans seemed to be female:

> He is at ease in all circumstances; he very rarely gets rattled ... Even in a world of mediocrities there must be a chief mediocrity ... Gay Byrne is the complete showman, the most astute and pleasing pro-fessional in the business. Reading over this piece, I find it most am-biguous. Did I praise him or blame him? I set out to castigate and

ended up hedging my bets. Why? I can't stand him. I abhor him. The poet in me demands a better programme for our put-upon people.[13]

Hartnett was a fervent believer in regional radio: 'People are more concerned with the local, the immediate, the contingent. One "night of the big wind" is worth more than a hundred earthquakes in China. Sad, in a way. But that is the human condition.'[14]

He described his situation in Templeglantine: 'Picture me, a blow-in to a rural community whose desires are basic: they want food, warmth, sex, drink, tobacco and news. And there am I, resident bi-lingual scarecrow, knowing Irish and English, listening to the news on Radio na Gaeltachta.' Hartnett describes the scene. He is tuned in to the Irish-speaking Radio na Gaeltachta and is translating the news for some neighbours who have called in to his 'rambling house'. 'Radio cannot survive unless it becomes regional. I listen. My neighbours listen. I translate.' He outlined what he thought his neighbours wanted from their radio stations:

> They don't want pop or plastic. They don't want invented causes. They want to hear about themselves. They don't want to hear a politician not answering a question. They don't want to hear bishops, cardinals and queens saying they 'regret' and they 'deplore'. They know the game. 'Whoops,' a government says, 'sorry we tortured people. We won't use these methods again.' 'Whoops,' the economist says, 'there is a shortage of coffee, so we will raise the price.' As if raising the price increases the supply. The people – the peasants they are called to make the proletariat feel superior – are wise. They have always been wise. Give them Radio na Gaeltachta. Give them regional radio. Death to the Top Twenty.[15]

It is not perhaps surprising that Hartnett did not last long as radio critic for *Hibernia*; less than a year in fact.

Besides his self-imposed banishment from English, Hartnett enjoyed many features of his rural retreat, in the early days at least. According to a newspaper report: 'The still of a summer night or winter nights with a bad-tempered wind lashing the land, will find poet Michael Hartnett creating in his hill-side cottage, with his family bedded down for the night.'[16] Hartnett practised his craft in Irish: 'As he looked out over the rolling green fields he mused, "I like it here, it's gentle and relaxing and I have no ambition to leave it physically, but I have to expand in the poetic sense".'

Friends recall his cooking skills. A much-thumbed copy of *Larousse Gastronomique* was his bible. He had always claimed that he was a 'chef manqué'. Nuala Ní Dhomhnaill remembered how he cooked a meal for her to celebrate her thirtieth birthday, the meal topped off with 'his very own homemade elderflower champagne'.[17]

In an article for the American tourist market Hartnett outlined some of the other delights of his local county:

Limerick City … has some excellent pubs and restaurants – but there is one item, which when I see it in a butcher's shop window makes me want to flee. It is the local delicacy, packet and tripe. Packet is a blood-pudding and looks like the partially decomposed member of a jackass and indeed, when cooked with the glutinous grey tripe, probably tastes like one.

And then there was *poitín*:

I was once given a quart of same, said to have been distilled in the Doon area. It had been aged and was equal in taste and bouquet to any Highland malt. Alas I over-indulged (a dangerous thing to do) and discovered that there are pookas, banshees and leprechauns in Ireland![18]

By 1978, after three years intermittent labour, Hartnett had completed his first collection of poetry in Irish. It was to be called *Adharca Broic* (which means 'badger's horns'; that is, something that doesn't exist), and to be published by The Gallery Press. Peter Fallon of The Gallery Press had been anxious to publish new material by Hartnett but his preference was for work in both languages. Before this, Gallery had not published Irish poetry. Fallon wrote to Hartnett in 1977: 'I asked if you might supply English versions of Badger's Horns and I think you wouldn't? Am I right? I'd be very interested in publishing a new book by you but I'd especially like it to be half-Irish, half English.'[19]

Fallon was acutely aware of Hartnett's renunciation of English and, from the tone of the letter, it seemed he expected a negative response. In 1976, he had wanted to include some of Hartnett's work in a proposed Gallery Press anthology. 'In the light of your "Farewell ..." this is perhaps a strange hope. I'd gladly acknowledge that these are not newer poems ...'[20]

Fallon then tried a slightly different tack, conscious as he was of the commercial limitations of books of Irish poetry: 'I wonder if you'd consider including translations/versions by you or by someone else. I would imagine that it would be possible to find a sympathetic and able friend.'[21]

Again Hartnett declined, and it wasn't as if he didn't have options. Liam Miller of The Dolmen Press, his first publisher, had been back in touch to tell him 'the doors are open'. However, Miller also pointed out: 'My policy on publishing in Irish is "only the best". We have only two books in Irish on our list. *An Béal Bocht* and *Cúirt an Mhean Oiche*.'[22]

165

In 1977, Gallery, in conjunction with Deerfield Press of Massachusetts, published a limited edition of 250 copies of two Hartnett poems in English, 'Maiden Street Wake' and the title poem 'Prisoners'. The book included the note, 'These poems were written before his declaration that he would henceforth write only in Irish, and have not previously appeared in print.'[23] His publishers were anxious not to appear to be undermining Hartnett's commitment.

Paul Durcan, in a letter to Hartnett, gave an account of the reaction of poetry fans in Northern Ireland who were puzzled at Hartnett's abandonment of English. 'All appear to have an intense and genuine curiosity (in the good sense) in what you are attempting. All are for you writing in Irish; but some genuinely cannot comprehend why you felt it necessary to bid farewell to English.' That was the general reaction, even of those who were sympathetic to the poet – puzzled bewilderment. Not only that, there were many poetry fans in Ireland who simply could not read Hartnett's new poetry; their Irish wasn't good enough. Durcan himself confessed to Hartnett, 'Irish, which once I could read, and even speak a little, is buried ten fathoms of bones inside me.'[24] Hugh McFadden had also spoken to Hartnett about his difficulty in understanding the poems in Irish, and Hartnett suggested helpfully that McFadden study Irish and soon he would be fluent enough.

Seán Lysaght appreciated the effort involved. 'Michael's mastery of Gaelic was not that of the native speaker; his was a work of research into a lost culture, a tradition betrayed.'[25] Eoghan Ó hAnluain took a different line. Like many he hoped that Hartnett's gesture was temporary: '"A Farewell to English" was a successful poem, a necessary genuflection towards the Gaelic tradition but not a binding legal contract.'[26]

Hartnett's old mentor, John Jordan, made the same point.

> The use of the indefinite article ['*A* Farewell to English'] allowed him an option (if the public requires that poets be moral dogmatists), I still think it does despite the fact that as recently as October 9th 1977, at the North Cork Writers' Festival, Doneraile, he re-iterated his commitment, total and poignant.[27]

Whatever was happening with his poetry, Hartnett appeared content with his rural existence:

> Although I feel one hundred per cent a country-man, I see on reflection that I have spent only seven of my thirty-six years actually living in the countryside … So being a countryman is, in my case, a state of mind, like being middle class … My rural vocation and my urban domicile have at least given me an insight into the differences between the countryman, the townsman, and the city dweller. Ireland is divided into those three classes: the other divisions, upper, middle, lower are arbitrary, paper divisions. Small-town people are the same, in almost every way as their country cousins, except their pool of knowledge and accomplishment is smaller … West Limerick is fortunate. Bord Fáilte have not discovered it, so its inhabitants do not have to play the part of countrymen …
>
> The one social phenomenon that really distinguishes the two life-styles is the funeral. The city dweller's area of friendship, acquaintanceship and relationship is much more limited than the countryman's … A city funeral is a matter of a few motor-cars and 'no flowers please'. The country funeral is an *aonach*, an assembly … The country funeral is a consolidation of roots and relationships … the event is a social one as well as a display of grief and respect. Old men meet old men. The tribe comes together …
>
> I am not for a moment saying that the countryman is in any

way superior to the city dweller. It's just that I prefer his way of life. I believe his values are important. I believe he is wiser, more tolerant and friendlier. I believe he reflects very clearly the mores of a supposedly vanished Gaelic society which is not like Dublin society, New York society or London society – all of which are the same.[28]

As he put it in one of his radio columns, 'City people are no longer a tribe. They have no totems, no gods.'[29]

16

'A Conspiracy of One'

In the run-up to the publication of *Adharca Broic*, his first collection since his switch to Irish, Hartnett was apprehensive of how it might be received. In an interview with Brian McLaughlin of *The Irish Press* Hartnett had stated his objective:

> The Irish language is like a rat and I would like to be the terrier who picks it up by the neck and shakes it, but I must avoid being bitten. I don't want to be made staid or complacent by campaigns or committees.[1]

Later he told McLaughlin:

> It's an important book for me and also a dangerous one. I have invited the suspicions of both the Anglo-Irish and the Gaelic cliques – the first because I have abandoned the Anglo-Irish medium, the second because I am not a native Irish speaker. I am not a *Gaeilgeoir* and I simply love the language and can express myself in that tongue more clearly than any other.[2]

But there was a residual air of hurt among the writers in English. Even John Jordan could not resist taking a swipe, referring to a time when he was Michael Hartnett not Mícheál Ó hAirtnéide, 'before he bade farewell to the deplorable, worn-out, leprous, unchaste English tongue'.[3]

Hartnett was full of plans and ideas and told McLaughlin that *Adharca Broic* was to be translated into Greek, German and Japanese. Also, he was busily engaged as the official poet to the Knight of Glin, which involved translating the volumes of poetry written about the family. As McLaughlin described it, 'Midnight and the waking hours sees the poet Hartnett spinning and weaving new metaphors in the foothills of Sliabh Luachra.'[4]

Hartnett was also denying that he was in any way a pioneer of any sort of movement:

> In one way I am contradicting myself. Even though I am not a flag-bearer, the very fact that I am getting them published in other languages, will make other peoples aware of the Irish language and in that sense I am a propagandist.[5]

His first collection of poems in Irish was three years in the making and was launched in the Central Hotel in Newcastle West in December 1978. The book was dedicated to five friends: Liam Brady, the Dublin musician, Pádraig Ó Fiannachta, Professor of Irish at Maynooth, Máirtín Ó Direáin, the poet, Mícheál Ó Ciarmhaic from Ballinskelligs and his old lover, Caitlín Maude, who had by then carved out a name for herself as a *sean-nós* singer, as well as an actor and a poet. At the launch RTÉ's Seán Mac-Reamoinn read some extracts from the poems. Present also was Denis Harnett, the poet's father, in a wheelchair; it was his first day out after a serious leg operation.

Hartnett told *The Irish Times* that he was working on a translation of some Gaelic poems that were 500 years old and written for members of the family of the Knight of Glin. He was also planning to write a play on the life and times of Aindrias Mac-Craith the eighteenth-century Croom poet.

Rosemary Hartnett felt somewhat excluded by her husband's new direction:

> Michael's decision to write only in Irish shut me out from his work. I had been accustomed to being the first to see his new work. I had tried to learn Irish but found it impossible. I couldn't access a night class, I bought the *Buntús Cainte* books and tried to study at home with Michael's help but he proved a very pedantic teacher. Whilst I was struggling with pronunciation, he would demonstrate the accents of the various different Gaeltachts for me, leaving me more baffled and frustrated. My daughter said I was attempting to speak Irish with a French accent! Worse, a series of Irish-speaking visitors called to the house and spent the whole evening with Michael conversing in Gaelic. Any attempt to enter the conversation in English was rebuffed. I retired defeated and angry from my struggles with the language.[6]

The reaction of contemporary critics to *Adharca Broic* was not entirely enthusiastic. 'Rumours (not without foundation) that his grasp of Irish grammar was less than secure, diverted the attention of his natural audience, Irish speakers, from the progressive nature of his poetry in Irish.'[7] Dennis O'Driscoll said that:

> his verse is rather less complex in construction and less resonant in vocabulary as yet than his English work. But his command of Irish is already equal to the demands of love and indignation and capable of evoking above all a pre-Christian and still savage world ... poems of his standard are a more forceful incentive for learning to understand the Irish language than patriotic or political ones.[8]

However, part of the challenge Hartnett had set himself was that he would be judged by the highest standards in what was, essentially, his second language. Owing to the well-publicised theatrical nature of his farewell to his first language there was little danger that he would be overlooked. Louis de Paor said:

> That his poems should have been critiqued from the outset by the best-known and most demanding critics is in itself a testament to his standing with the editors of the various journals in which his work was reviewed and indeed with the critics themselves who judged him, as was only fitting, against the high standards he had set himself by his work in English.[9]

De Paor also argued that:

> Given the political and cultural climate of the mid-1970s, the decision to turn his back on an already established reputation in English in favour of a language whose literary capital appeared to be on the brink of insolvency was to wilfully court obscurity and oblivion.[10]

But notwithstanding that, 'considering the straitened circumstances in which it was published the achievement of Ó hAirtnéide's debut volume in Irish, *Adharca Broic*, is nothing short of extraordinary'.[11]

Tomás Ó Floinn, perhaps the most eminent critic in the Irish language at the time, applauded the poet's courage and artistic integrity, but found *Adharca Broic* an uneven collection.

While writing the collection, Hartnett taught for a time at Thomond College of Education in Limerick, but it was not to last, even though they were happy with his work, as can be seen in the letter from Hugh O'Donnell, head of the English department, dated 30 May 1978:

To Whom it Concerns

Michael Hartnett has been a part-time member of the English Department of Thomond College of Education for the academic years 1976/77 and 1977/78. He has developed and participated in the following programmes, Introduction to Poetry, Introduction to English Poetry, Anglo-Irish Poetry and Creative Writing.

His contribution to these areas has been highly valued by the English Department. This is particularly so in relation to the Creative Writing programmes where his students have benefited in a special way from his own acknowledged work as one of the important contemporary poets in Ireland at the present time. His presence on the Campus has been an enriching one and has generated considerable interest in poetry and writing among his students.

I have no hesitation in recommending Michael Hartnett for any position where the above experience will be of relevance. It is my hope that he will not have to break the ties he has forged with Thomond College.[12]

According to Rosemary Hartnett, 'Michael stopped his stint at Thomond because we were planning to move to Cork City ... He solicited work from UCC but it did not materialise because he had no degree.'[13]

Nuala Ní Dhomhnaill, newly returned from Turkey, was impressed by the bravery of Hartnett's decision to write in Irish:

It was electrifying. It made me feel that my arse-over-head decision to give up a 'proper job', sell my furniture to buy the plane tickets home, break up the family and drag my children 3,000 miles away to another language in West Kerry might be worth it after all.[14]

In fact, so impressed was she by his gesture that she sought him out in his Templeglantine retreat.

It was just as well I had left myself a few hours to do so because to my complete discombobulation there were more than three Michael Hartnetts in the vicinity ... By a dogged process of questions and answers I finally found the house to the left of a narrow road, over a hump-backed bridge and walked into a kitchen where I introduced myself ... I felt I should have said 'Michael Hartnett, I presume'. I was as overawed as Stanley must have felt when he discovered Livingstone.[15]

According to Ní Dhomhnaill, 'for someone who had a well-developed and recognisable voice in English, to throw it to the winds did seem a bit wilful at the very least', and she felt that 'he got little thanks from the established writers of either language for this enormous sacrifice'.[16] She wondered at the wisdom of giving up 'an accomplished and sophisticated voice in English for another language, and one which was so hedged around with a barbed wire of shibboleth-strewing-pundits and political agendas that made it difficult to produce anything new':[17]

[What he] gave up by switching to Irish was inestimable. It was not made any easier for him by snide comments from his peers in English, one who couldn't resist the easy jibe from Dickens, 'nothing so much became him in this life as his leaving of it.'[18]

The Irish language critics were no easier on him: 'I could have told him myself about the bile of the professional "Gaeilgeoirs" who were ever so quick to pounce on the cheeky impieties of us "*na filí óga*/the young poets" who were trying to do something new'.[19] She was of the opinion that his Irish 'was very much an emanation of the man himself, dapper, formal in a slightly old-fashioned way, eminently literary'.[20]

There was still a suspicion among Irish language writers that Hartnett would not remain writing solely in that language. In 1979, Donal MacAmhlaigh reported in *The Irish Press* a discussion he had overheard when an Irish poet had asked: 'Do you think will Hartnett ever go back to English?' The reply was, 'He will, to be sure, no matter how well he writes in Irish because not to do so would be like giving up the use of one arm.'[21]

In 1979 The Gallery Press published a slightly longer version of *A Farewell to English*. In an Editor's Note, Peter Fallon explained that the enlarged edition included other poems pre-dating Hartnett's resolution, many of them unpublished and uncollected, and gave some commentators the chance to review it again. Dennis O'Driscoll, in *Hibernia*, felt that:

> the additional poems make it a far more balanced and satisfying collection and the attractive Gaelic strain evident in the poems makes one wish he could have behaved more promiscuously, continuing to court his old English muse as well as his new Guaranteed Irish one.[22]

However, as Gréagóir Ó Dúill pointed out:

> The border country between the two languages can be inhospitable. Hartnett and Ó Tuairisc, even Ó Riordain before them, found the Irish language market ultra-conservative, given to the wagging finger of the conservative language purist, scrupulous as to grammar and syntax and traditional norms.[23]

Hartnett had promised The Gallery Press a collection of poems called *Daoine*. He received an advance, but when he missed his deadline he offered to repay it. Peter Fallon wrote in July 1980: 'Don't dare return the advance.'[24] He was willing to wait.

Hartnett made the odd, infrequent appearance on poetry programmes on RTÉ and made a good impression on some of his listeners. Mary Leland of *The Irish Times* felt that 'Michael Hartnett is one of the most attractive occasional contributors to radio in Ireland …'[25] In 1979, RTÉ asked him to take over as presenter of *Poems Plain* on Radio 1, to replace Seamus Heaney who was going to the United States. The fifteen-minute programmes were recorded in RTÉ's Limerick studios, and the fee for the programme was £40, rising to £45 later. For a man with a young family and no steady income, the money was much appreciated.

Mary Leland was quite taken by Hartnett's presenting skills. 'Michael Hartnett's programme is alive with his own response to poetry of all kinds … then he tells you about his findings in a rapid determined voice alight with the pleasures he has discovered.'[26] But Mary Lappin of *The Irish Press* was less of a fan: 'Hartnett made his debut with a laboured, albeit scrupulously conscientious analysis of "Sam's Cross", a Paul Durcan offering …'[27] Lappin considered Hartnett's choice of subjects too esoteric for his presumed audience. His programme on the concept that poets are the unacknowledged legislators of the world, particularly raised her ire. Brecht, Machado, Lorca, Eluard and Pasternak were among the poets covered; too out of the ordinary, in her opinion, for a programme entitled *Poems Plain*. In a later column she reported that 'I was gently chided by Michael Hartnett for having questioned his wisdom by including works by exotic poets of the Cavafy and Mayakovsky genre in a series allegedly treating of *Poems Plain*. I'm not a whit repentant':[28]

Why don't I like Hartnett? His work invariably gives the impression of being laboured, as if the *mot juste* doesn't come readily to him. His criticism is occasionally too cannibalistic, his praise sometimes too niggardly and his choice of subject matter frequently infelicitous. I honestly can't visualise the average listener giving a tinker's curse about the poetry of Hermann Hesse or about the editorial acumen of J. A. Richards.[29]

Hartnett was replaced at short notice by Seamus Deane in September 1980, and was quite upset. Aside from everything else, he needed a regular income. Mary Leland missed him:

> There's chaos in every direction and I'm not able for it. Where is Michael Hartnett? I'm quite prepared to welcome Seamus Deane, who wouldn't be? to *Poems Plain* … but surely I'm permitted to miss the dips and swoops of Hartnett's voice and to wonder what has happened.[30]

Even Mary Lappin questioned his abrupt departure from the airwaves. 'Although I've never been a Michael Hartnett aficionado, my sense of fair play was outraged at the apparent cavalier treatment meted out to him when his ongoing *Poems Plain* stint was abruptly terminated.'[31]

In 1979 Gabriel Fitzmaurice first met Michael Hartnett while he was working for Listowel Writers' Week and was director of its ballad programme. 'I travelled to Michael's house in Templeglantine to invite him to adjudicate the competition. He, a ballad lover himself, readily agreed.'[32] Hartnett had a long association with Listowel Writers' Week and with John B. Keane whose family often gave him accommodation for the duration of the festival.

Hartnett was also very active in the arts scene in Newcastle West, as was his wife Rosemary, who for a time was chairperson of the Arts Committee. Poets were invited down to do readings.

Some were more successful than others, as Vincent Buckley found out:

> One day in 1981 ... Michael Hartnett rang me up from Newcastle West ... and asked would I read there. What pay would I ask? I didn't know and said so and was surprised when Michael mentioned £80 ... He would read with me, unpaid and local musicians would play.[33]

Buckley found Hartnett:

> an amusingly intense man ... I was to read in the building that gives the town its name, the banqueting hall of the now destroyed castle of the Fitzgeralds, Earls of Desmond ... The hall is very handsome, but very dilapidated ... you read seated in a stone window embrasure; the acoustics are excellent; the possibilities are great ...

However, at the appointed hour, nobody had turned up. Buckley repaired to Lynch's bar next to the hall. 'Every so often Gabriel [Fitzmaurice] would enter, looking fierce ... and Michael would enter looking quite distracted ... An hour and a half after starting-time, I said to him, What does it matter, Michael? Let's call it off. I don't mind.' But Hartnett was adamant that it would go ahead and eventually it did. By his recollection, Buckley performed to an audience of about a dozen, 'whom I read at, as vigorously as I could'. Buckley offered to forego his fee, but Hartnett was resolute. It was a point of honour with him that he had promised a payment. He went from pub to pub and made a collection to raise the money. Buckley concluded that the people of Newcastle West 'were far more interested in the idea of poetry than in the reality ... Poetry was treated with reverence and neglect ...'[34] According to Gabriel Fitzmaurice, there was a simpler explanation for what had happened, which was 'that Michael had mistakenly advertised the reading for the following night'.[35]

Hartnett's following collections in Irish betrayed a marked decline in his outlook. The easy optimism of his initial conversion to Irish had long faded:

> I dislike the dead
> And avoid the living
> My friends disagree with me
> And I with them
> And when I read today's poetry
> I laugh forests of pens
> And cry tears of ink
>
>
> Critics have no interest in me
> I have no contact with my friends
> A man forgotten by literature
> A bastard, a loner
> The Gaels are suspicious of me
> And the Galls think I'm out of my mind.[36] [*translation from the Irish*]

Dennis O'Driscoll asked Hartnett about the negative nature of the poems.

> Your poem, 'An Phurgóid', seems to have stemmed from a crisis of language?

> I was dissatisfied with not just my version of the Irish language. I wanted to write a poetry which contained no adjectives and no allusions. I found that worked, up to a point. I was almost taking a Beckettian stance of writing a poem which would have one

syllable. That was at the end of a 10-year period of writing in Irish exclusively.[37]

The poem illustrated his isolation and his feeling that he had been rejected by the Irish-speaking critics at the time:

> I'm a conspiracy of one.
> I'm humble, arrogant; when all is done
> my rules are easily broken.[38]
> [*English translation, Gabriel Fitzmaurice*]

With time, Hartnett grew more bitter and more self-critical. He had never been a fan of literary critics despite the fact that he had been a rigorous poetry reviewer for *The Irish Times*, *The Irish Press* and *Hibernia* in the early 1970s: 'The poet is his own best reader, for a start. The second best reader is the reader himself.' As for the critics, they were the worst readers: 'They very rarely discuss what you have written, but what you should have written.'[39] He outlined the philosophy that was the basis of his own criticism:

> A critic of any genre, if he is worth the space he takes up on paper, must have a preconceived notion of what the ideal he's striving towards must be. This, of course, leads at worst to dictatorship and eventual sterility via repetition or toward total chaos if the critic is just working tongue in cheek, and at best towards the realisation of his ideal which again may not be everybody's cup of tea. All criticism tends towards conversion: All poet-critics want all poets to comply with their own notion of what a poem should be, for instance.[40]

Alan Titley, for one was impressed: '*An Phurgóid*, full of fire, anger, argumentation and verbal agility is the best long poem in Irish written in the last ten years.'[41] He sympathised with Hartnett's situation:

> The bilingual writer in Ireland runs the danger of being treated with suspicion by both traditions without gaining the entire respect of either. We sometimes like to whip our writers into parties to make manageable critical fodder of them, but fortunately, the best will always resist this even if they are misunderstood in the process. Whatever bolts Michael Hartnett had shot in English he drove them home when he turned to Irish … His poetry is not the kind that can be stuffed and mounted and admired from a distance. At his best he challenges us to attack and defeat the bland, to out the truth from behind the great simplicities, and that is as worthy a way to feed the world as anything else.[42]

With the publishing of his *Collected Poems*, Volume 1 (in English) in 1984, Hartnett still professed his defiance:

> In my case the poems in English constitute a corpus. My efforts in this language, as far as poetry is concerned, are now ended. I am still at the apprentice stage in Gaelic and sometimes despair when I read the works of other poets – but I intend to write on and I learn … Many of the English poems express my uneasiness and indicate a movement towards Gaelic.

He believed his poems were 'a kind of psychic autobiography and they echo with past emotional states. They are a diary where many bitter truths are made palatable by as many pretty lies – not to deceive the reader but to comfort the writer.'

However, John F. Deane questioned the very idea of a 'collected' version of Hartnett at this stage of his career:

I am not convinced of the value of issuing Hartnett now in a 'Collected' state. His decision to write only in Irish has always seemed to me to be based on somewhat romantic notions, and a reading of his collected verse serves to convince me that this is true, that indeed he is an unwilling romantic poet. The decisions of a poet must surely be allowed to reside in the present tense of his development as a poet; the issuing of a collected works states this is not so.[43]

Deane was one of those who hoped that Hartnett would return to writing in English.

The determination to write no more in English is put forward in poetry that is so mature and powerful as to need no more reasons for its own existence than that, no matter what it states. There are many of us fondly (?) hoping he will change his mind ... there is a very wide and appreciative readership longing for him to 'come back' to English poetry.[44]

Brendan Kennelly in his review of Hartnett's *Collected Poems* was sympathetic to the poet's plight, though he had more questions than answers:

I've read notes and articles about Hartnett's dilemma: was he wise to say farewell to English? Was he foolish to abandon a language in which he had frequently shown a confident lightness of touch, achieved a lyrical density that was often startlingly rich in its statements and implications, haunting us with rhythms that took something from Irish ballads and mingled it with his reading of European poetry? Did he know Irish in the only way possible for someone who wishes to write in that language, that is, did he know it in his blood as well as in his mind? These questions, and others, were asked. The answers came too, only they weren't the real answers, because the real answers have yet to be discovered.[45]

Kennelly was an admirer of Hartnett's passionate nature:

This tendency to write in sequences is evidence of that obsessive quality in Hartnett's imagination which I mentioned earlier. Obsessiveness can be boring, even sick, in life; in poetry it can be a powerful force, teasing out oppositions and alternatives, setting up apparent absolutes only to scuttle them, establishing ideas and beliefs as authentic only to accuse them of pretence or even fraudulence.[46]

Kennelly concluded his review with some warm words of advice:

A Farewell to English is a public statement of a private artistic intention. 'I have made my choice and leave with little weeping/I have come with meagre voice to court the language of my people.' Hartnett may court that language. He may even love it. He has already had a few healthy children by the union. But will he stay till death do them part? My own guess is that he will write in both Irish and English. And why not? There are many partitions in Ireland and the political one is by no means the deepest. I've seen and heard a lot of stupid bitterness voiced on both sides of the linguistic divide. Michael Hartnett, as man and artist, is, to my knowledge and belief, devoid of this futile, corrosive thing. He is a poet who wants to create good poems in whichever language comes to him. He should forget about allegiance to either and gladly accept the gifts of both. The truest allegiance a writer can pay to a language is to use it well.[47]

17

'POET CAUSES MAYHEM WITH SALAD SAGA'

In 1980, Hartnett organised a local publication by the Observer Press of a poem in English, 'Maiden Street Ballad' (it had originally had the working title 'Mike Hartnett's Ballad'). It had the dedication, 'This ballad was composed by Michael Hartnett in Glendarragh, Templeglantine, County Limerick in the month of December 1980 as a Christmas present for his father Denis Harnett.' It had a limited run, being an old-fashioned nostalgic ballad set to the air of 'The Limerick Rake'. In the booklet itself the text was supplemented by old photographs of the Maiden Street area supplied by the Newcastle West Local History society. As Hartnett put it in one of the early verses: 'A poet's not a poet until the day he/can write a few songs for his people'.

In the preface to the ballad Hartnett wrote of his affection for his home place:

> Everyone has a Maiden Street. It is the street of strange characters, wits, odd old women and eccentrics: also a street of hot summers, of hop-scotch and marbles: in short the street of youth. But Maiden Street was no Tír na nÓg ... Human warmth and poverty often go hand in hand ... The object of this ballad is to invoke and preserve 'times past' and to do so without being too sentimental ... But this ballad is not all grimness. I hope it is humorous in spots. It was not

written with mockery but with affection – part funny song, part so-cial history.[1]

At the beginning of his 'Maiden Street Ballad' Hartnett professed his defiance of his detractors, that the poem was intended for one person's eyes only: 'If the critics don't like it they can all kiss my arse/as long as it's read by my father'.

While he was aware of the dangers of sentimentality, Hartnett was not prone to nostalgia: 'but if you think you can go back then you are a fool/for the past is signposted "No Entry".'

A large part of the ballad dealt with the pubs of Newcastle West and its surrounding area. Hartnett claimed that the cement that bound the Irish people together was not religion or patriot-ism, but porter.[2] Pubs for him were a refuge 'when from wife or from weather I am forced to hide'. Pubs had always been a large part of his life. Perhaps, now that he had more time on his hands, they became more so. Reminiscing on his past, he was thankful for his freedom:

> Sunday morning is for me the most pleasurable morning of the week … I am lucky I suppose not to be cursed and patterned by the tyr-anny of the five-day week or by the consideration that Sunday after all is a religious day. In the last few years my children's church-going proclivities have brought hundreds of blurry Sundays back into focus … In Dublin when I was a 'student', a solemn, fragile pilgrimage to McDaid's for a cure: next London – same pilgrimage, different pub. Back in Dublin from 1968 to 1974 I did the state some service as a Male Night Telephonist when Sunday differed from the other days of the week in that there were very few alarm calls on that morning.[3]

'Maiden Street Ballad' was not the only poem in English that Hartnett wrote during his self-imposed banishment from the language. His angry denunciation 'Who Killed Bobby Sands?' was written in 1981. In 1983, a single-sheet poem, 'The Ballad of Salad Sunday', attributed to 'The Wasp', was distributed around Newcastle West. Hartnett did not make much effort to disguise its authorship. Martin Byrnes of *The Limerick Echo* reported on 6 August 1983, in the front-page story headlined 'Poet Causes Mayhem with Salad Saga':

> An internationally renowned poet has caused merry mayhem in his native town. Michael Hartnett has published a scathing ballad telling of a monumental blunder made by many shopkeepers and publicans some weeks ago. The lampoon recalls the occasion of the Circuit of Munster Rally, based in the town. Many traders prepared piles of salads and sandwiches to sell to the expected throngs. But the throngs never came, so the shopkeepers were left eating stale sandwiches and wilting lettuce for a week … Just when the shop people believed that their egg-on-face day had been forgotten, Michael Hartnett produced his tongue-in-cheek reminder … In the tradition of the wandering poets of old, he hawked his pamphlet around the town, asking 20p per copy … Hundreds of copies of the ballad were snapped up in the first couple of days … One unnamed publican said, 'He's gone a bit too far. We'd have preferred to forget it.'[4]

Hartnett felt that the poem was in the tradition of bards such as John Ahern and Danny Barry, who had written satirical poems. He believed he may even have been 'barred' from one particular pub because of the ballad.

Hartnett, as ever, was full of ideas for new projects. He told Byrnes that as well as translating Ó Bruadair he was working on a book of Celtic cookery, had begun his memoirs, and was writing the libretto of an opera based on his work 'Cúlú Ide'. At the behest of the politician and local historian, Jim Kemmy, Hartnett wrote a number of articles for the *Old Limerick Journal*, though some were effectively reprints of material that had already appeared in *The Irish Times*, dealing with his childhood in Newcastle West.

In notes that he made for a creative writing workshop to be run at Listowel Writers' Week in 1983, Hartnett outlined his literary values. There were four phases to a poet's career:

1. The Apprentice Phase characterised by 'borrowing, practising forms ...'
2. The Competent Phase, in which ... the critics accept it, the poets accept it, the nation accepts it ... there is much repetition ...
3. The Purging Phase ... the most difficult phase, in which the poet has to abandon years of training, the belief in belief, here comes the walk-out, abandoning all you have learnt except language itself ...
4. The Plateau Phase ... where the poet has no allies but himself, his own soul and mind, his own ideas ... he must create a new philosophy, new metaphors ... the philosophy may not be valid (what philosophy is?) but it must be his.[5]

Hartnett ran various workshops for Listowel Writers' Week over the years. As he told *The Kerryman* in 1983, 'It opens peoples' eyes and helps them to properly evaluate what they are writing. The workshop helps them to become better poets and writers. It encourages them.' He added that the workshop was particularly beneficial to writers who were working in virtual isolation as it helped them to achieve a sense of purpose and a common goal with other writers.[6]

Hartnett may not have seen the English poems from this period as entirely 'serious'. When they were actually collected in later years, they were published under the title *A Book of Strays*. Hartnett suggested the label.

By this time Rosemary Hartnett had taken up work as Welfare

Officer in the personnel department of Aughinish Alumina. One of her main tasks was to help the families of the 4,000 workers who were new to the area to integrate into the community. As someone who had been a newcomer to West Limerick herself, less than ten years before, she could appreciate their problems. As she told the *Irish Independent*:

> we must avoid a ghetto for the wives and families. They are not obliged to join in the social activities but we encourage them in fact to join clubs and organisations … the fact that I lived in other countries gave me an insight into what people are looking for in a country … Generally when people anywhere move into a major new project like this, they have to flounder around and find their own way, which can take a long time. But already there is a fine camaraderie building up which everyone is very enthusiastic about.[7]

In October 1984, Hartnett's father Denis died. Their relationship had always been difficult. 'My father played a great part in my life. I was his first son. I saw him in good times and bad.'[8] In 'That Actor Kiss' he wrote of the relationship:

> He willed to me his bitterness and thirst,
> his cold ability to close a door.

He described in the poem how he had kissed his father as he lay in his hospital bed:

> Later, over a drink, I realised,
> that was our last kiss and, alas our first.[9]

18

'MY ENGLISH DAM BURSTS'

Hartnett's *Collected Poems*, Volume 1, published in 1984, contained the stark dedication: 'For Rosemary, whom I do not deserve'. At this stage, his marriage was in difficulty. His wife was worried about the effect his drinking was having on their children:

> The cause of the breakup had everything to do with alcoholism and its effect on family life. Michael became moody, unreliable and bad-tempered. There was an inability to distinguish truth from fiction in his everyday life. He embarrassed and sometimes frightened his children. He was no longer repentant after his drinking bouts. He denied that he had a problem and refused to consider treatment. He justified all his actions by saying that he was a poet and drinking was part of him and necessary for writing.[1]

Hartnett himself seemed surprised by the break-up:

> The elaborate structures we built up –
> the house, the children and the plastered walls,
> the crystal and the willow-pattern cup –
> now fall, as my small shabby façade falls.[2]

In 1984, after the break-up, he moved back to Dublin to live in a working-class area of the city. The following year marked his return to mainstream English publications with *Inchicore Haiku*, a book that deals with the turbulent events in his personal life over the previous few years. As he put it:

> My English dam bursts,
> And out stroll all my bastards
> Irish shakes its head.[3]

Dermot Bolger, whose Raven Arts Press published *Inchicore Haiku*, believed Hartnett's social seclusion exacerbated his drinking. 'Alone in Ireland while his family were on an extended visit to Australia, Michael seemed to drift into the engulfing tide of alcohol.'[4] Before *Inchicore Haiku* there were two years when he couldn't write. Asked, 'What did you do?' Michael replied, 'Drink [*sic*].'[5]

Hartnett was apprehensive that people would see his return to English as a betrayal. In many ways critical reaction to his original decision had softened over time as people came to terms with it. Gerald Dawe, in his review of Hartnett's *Collected Poems* Volume 1 in the *Sunday Independent* in 1984, took the opportunity to examine what he stood for:

> Much of Michael Hartnett's *Collected Poems* deals with these matters – of the place poetry finds for itself in the life of a community, of the poet himself and where he stands in regards to the language he uses and underpinning these points is Hartnett's persistent sense of indignation, aggravated by what he sees as the inauthentic, the slick and the despoiling, here is too a recurrent sense of himself as a poet working out his own identity ... Hartnett is at his best in the short, compressed lyrical statement in which he addresses the poet's traditional questioning of society's values.[6]

In the same review Dawe described *A Farewell to English* as 'that

most compelling and convincing of recent poetic manifestoes …
It is a brave stand and excellent poetry.'

The eighty-seven haikus of *Inchicore Haiku* dealt with the realities of his solitary existence in his flat in Inchicore and his heavy drinking:

> Somewhere in the house
> a tap gushes out water
> – sounds of someone else

> My liver sneers up
> from the bottom of a glass
> snug in golden hell

> A pint of Guinness
> – black as my Catholic heart
> black as broken vows

> I drink my regrets
> mixed with a dash of bitters.
> My lungs smoke cancer.[7]

Some dealt with the political:

> From St Michael's Church
> the electric Angelus
> – another job gone

> What do bishops take
> when the price of bread goes up?
> A vow of silence.

Along Emmet Road
politician's promises
blow like plastic bags.[8]

Others illustrated his homesickness:

On a brick chimney
I can see all West Limerick
in a jackdaw's eye.

My beloved hills
my family and my friends
– my empty pockets

Blackbird, robin, thrush?
I cannot place the singer.
Exile blunts the ear.

Hartnett wrote of his guilt:

I learnt the hard way
acts of love can break a heart.
Seven white sea-gulls.

Dead faces watch me
– people I have wronged and loved.
Milk sours in the cup.

Banished for treason
for betraying my country
I live in myself.

Hartnett concluded *Inchicore Haiku* with a reference to his late father's defiant socialism:

All divided up,
all taught to hate each other.
'Are these my people?'

My dead father shouts
from his eternal Labour:
'These are your people!' [9]

As the haikus indicated, it was not a happy existence and, to give his life in Inchicore some structure, Hartnett made himself a timetable:

8.30	Rise, breakfast, shave
9.00	Write
12.00	Lunch
1–4	Write
4	Snack
4.15	Walk, shopping
6	Tea
6.30–8	Potter, read, think
8–10	Pub (if possible)
10	Home, read, supper[10]

He resolved to limit himself to a visit to the cinema once a week, and eight cigarettes a day.[11] Whether he held himself to these restrictions is another matter.

Hartnett had been apprehensive about people's reaction to his return to English but, in general, he should not have worried, as critical reaction was quite positive, and the new poems were judged on their own merits. Perhaps his vow mattered more to himself than it did to others. Peter Sirr in *The Irish Times*, while welcoming Hartnett's re-appearance, felt that the form he had chosen was too limiting to be totally successful:

> The haiku form has a somewhat dubious reputation in English language poetry. It lends itself to amateurish imagism and, more often than not, it offers less a real poetic challenge than a framework for banality. Hartnett … adapts the form freely to his own purposes … the images are particular, attentive, witty, the tone often gently sad or satirical, yet always open to the clatter of hope … To open any page is to come on the poet listening, observing, watching, waiting, adding to his diary of minutiae in which every entry implies, but keeps at bay, the larger gesture, the barer cry.[12]

Despite Hartnett's fears there were few recriminations. Some critics actually welcomed Hartnett's return to writing in English. Eamon Grennan was happy to see him back:

> Having left the high road of the English tradition … he has now come back to the English language along the absorbing bye-roads of translation and adaptation (*Inchicore Haiku* is an odd mixture of Oriental lyricism and social outrage with a Gaelic flavour).[13]

In one of his workbooks Hartnett wrote some notes to himself with regard to his poetry:

> It is necessary to be aware of tradition & influences but not to parade them. No allusions. No adjectives. No Poems ending Madrid 1963 or Sneem 1970 or Constantinople 1970, etc.
>
> Not Beckett. I don't want to dispense with form or emotion. I want to dispense with incest and embalming.

Critics/academics have a handful of tags by which they can recognise a 'poem'. They miss the subtleties or the badnesses.

Poems about poets, about poems, about literary characters, about music, painting, sculpture, about philosophy, psychiatry (other people's), about places (no place-names), about history, about religion(s). Problem: to get away from all that and still create poetry ...

A poet = his collected poems. What does he want to leave behind? No bohemia, no collected letters, no public lovers, no eccentricities ...[14]

19

'The Bible in Scouse'

Dermot Bolger was concerned for Hartnett's physical decline after his move back to Dublin: 'Within months he was living in a small bed-sit in Inchicore. His marriage was over. His face, which had never aged, was suddenly old and drawn. His chief defence against fate remained his sense of humour.'[1] *Inchicore Haiku* had been dedicated: 'For Angela Liston who saved my life'. Having begun a new relationship, Hartnett eventually moved into her basement flat on Dartmouth Road. Angela brought a certain structure to his life, as he was well aware. Hartnett thanked her in poem:

The rules you make,
the strictures you insist on
have made me a beggar before you,
Angela Liston.

I have been kicked around the place,
been mocked and have been pissed on,
but I find my way home to you,
Angela Liston.

And my wrinkled anxious forehead,
amazingly has been kissed on,
and I am blessed by you,
Angela Liston.[2]

Though Hartnett had resumed living in Dublin, writing in both English and Irish, he was in severe financial difficulties. He had debts to repay and did his best to make some money from his poetry. Now that Hartnett had returned to writing in English he settled down to complete his long delayed project: translating Dáibhí Ó Bruadair. He had come across Ó Bruadair's work at a young age, when an elderly inhabitant of his home town had recited some of his poetry. He had been fascinated by him ever since:

> It is not rare for a poet to be obsessed by the work and mind of another poet. The obsession can express itself in many ways – scorn (which is often public), awe before a massive superiority (which is always private), and love, which can become a bore to readers who do not share the obsession. I am obsessed by the work and mind of Dáibhí Ó Bruadair and, though I certainly love it and him, my obsession usually expresses itself in frustration. And it has done so since 1954 when I was thirteen.[3]

Hartnett researched Ó Bruadair's life, though there was little documentary evidence available, believing this research to be part of the translation process; to translate a poet you had to understand the conditions in which his poetry was written.

The Gallery Press had been waiting for a finished manuscript from Hartnett since the early 1980s, but Hartnett kept missing his deadlines. Ó Bruadair seemed to be an obsession. He was also working on it for his doctorate from Trinity College. He composed a variety of translations of some of Ó Bruadair's work and labelled them 'Literal', 'Standard', 'Metrical', 'Colloquial' and 'Tonal' translations, as if it was a technical exercise. It was little wonder that he missed so many deadlines.[4]

Ó Bruadair had lived through, and witnessed the collapse of
Gaelic society in the 1600s. In the old order, the professional poet
had been held in great esteem. Hartnett was in some ways envious
of the status of poets such as Ó Bruadair in his time: 'Patronage
was still deemed essential to a poet's survival: there were no
publishers, no royalties, no grants, there were gifts, hospitality,
cattle, horses, clothing and sometimes gold.'[5] However, with
the displacement of the Gaelic aristocracy so went the poet's
place in that system; his social status and spiritual authority was
diminished. Again Hartnett identified with Ó Bruadair's plight.
He felt isolated and ignored by modern Ireland.

Ó Bruadair had been a mass of contradictions. Poet and essay-
ist Chris Agee described Ó Bruadair as 'anti-English yet royalist,
Catholic yet anti-clerical, Gaelic-speaking yet profoundly out of
sympathy with the native Irish'.[6] Hartnett even defended Ó Bruadair's political and social attitudes which many had interpreted
as elitist snobbery:

> Ó Bruadair was certainly not a peasant. In fact he had little time for
> the peasantry, pausing only to mock their greed and slavish adoption
> of English ways … He was very much a contemporary poet, he com-
> mented with courage and conviction on the Ireland of his time: in
> fact none of his poems are about the past, though he uses history and
> genealogy to point his statements … Far greater than Ó Rathaille,
> who had lyricism which Ó Bruadair had not, except in rare mo-
> ments, bitterness they shared, but Ó Rathaille lacked one attribute
> which Ó Bruadair had, majesty.[7]

It is obvious that Hartnett identified with his precursor, the poet
as outsider:

Ó Bruadair could be funny, obscure and anguished. He had immense dignity and immense bitterness. If he is anti-democratic it is because he confused survival with betrayal. He was concerned with culture. He would not have liked the Ireland of the 1980s.[8]

Hartnett missed deadline after deadline with his publisher, The Gallery Press, perhaps as a result of his inclination to fiddle with his translations. He had always had strong views on the subject and particularly identified with Ó Bruadair's isolation from his society. As Thomas O'Grady, Professor of English and Director of Irish Studies at the University of Massachusetts, put it:

> this professional poet of the old Gaelic social order became the symbol of what he wanted to be. Not surprisingly, his selections … of his precursor's verse focus almost exclusively on the downward spiral of the presence – and the practice – of poetry in Irish society during the politically and culturally turbulent decades of the seventeenth century. As his version of 'Is Urchra Cléibh' (a lament written after the departure in 1692 of many of the Irish chieftains) reflects, Hartnett identifies especially with Ó Bruadair's perspective as beleaguered guardian of a noble art.[9]

Hartnett, in particular, empathised with Ó Bruadair's views on the decline of the status of poets in society.

> To see the art of poetry lost
> with those who honoured it with thought –
> its true form lowered to a silly chant,
> sought after by the dilettante.[10]

Feeling especially that many prominent Irish families, both English-speaking as well as Gaelic, had betrayed their traditional culture, the culture that sustained him as a professional poet, in not resisting more vigorously the colonising British juggernaut, in his later verse, Ó Bruadair appears more and more as a self-appointed lightning rod of conscience.[11]

Máirtín Ó Murchú of Trinity College Dublin, offered a private criticism of some of the translations:

> Michael Hartnett himself sometimes slips into a rather broad trans-lation ... I cannot agree that the colloquial mode is appropriate nor ultimately successful ... It is like the Bible in Scouse. It aligns Ó Bruadair with a type of speech register which is at variance with the role he had in the society of his day: he was a member of the native learned class, an aristocrat, and his speech reflects that (this does not prevent him from being impolite, abusive and earthy).[12]

Hartnett went to great lengths in his attempts to reproduce the authentic voice of the poet he was translating:

> Many would say that I have created an unnecessary and insurmount-able barrier between myself and Ó Bruadair in my insistence that a poet who is such a consummate craftsman should be translated with obsessive care, that his techniques should be brought across as faith-fully as possible. 'Poetry is that which gets lost in the translation' is a widely-held notion; I do not agree with it. A poet/translator, if he loves the original better than he loves himself, will get the poetry across; he may even get the whole poem across or, at second best, force his own version – within the strictures laid down by the original author – as close as possible to poetry.[13]

In an article for *The Irish Times*, Hartnett outlined the rules he felt should govern the art of translation:

The references to Gaelic, of course, reflect my own obsession. It will be understood that translations from any language into English or Gaelic are meant ... The translator of poetry must be a poet. The end product must be a poem. Loyalty must be to the original poet/poem; one must love the original more than the new version. The new poem must not be in the same style as the poet/translator's own works. It should reflect the technical dexterity of the original. It should be written in the same metre – when this metre suits the theme in the new language.[14]

Finding a modern voice for Ó Bruadair was 'as difficult as trying to find a "voice" for Milton in Chinese'. Hartnett did not wish to afflict the poet with his own voice: 'to do that, too much of what survives of the original in my versions would be distorted'. While acknowledging the work done by Rev. John Mac Erlean, a previous translator of Ó Bruadair, Hartnett was critical of his limitations. Mac Erlean was a Jesuit priest and a Victorian gentleman and had censored some of Ó Bruadair's verse:

The heavy Gaelic type, made almost Germanic-looking by Ó Bruadair's compound words, coupled with the leaden English of Mac Erlean's versions does not make the poet look attractive ... I resolved (in 1970) to translate him myself. Soon after, I thought my decision rash. I made many starts and stops. I read and re-read the poems.

In his introduction Hartnett quoted Mac Erlean's views:

All poetry suffers severely in the process of translation into a strange language. Many of those qualities which give charm to the verse in the original are incapable of reproduction in a different idiom ... Choiceness of expression and terseness of diction vanish, and with them harmony of phrase … It is difficult to translate any poetry tolerably; but Irish poetry is, admittedly, of all the most untranslatable … My chief aim throughout has been to make the translation as literal as possible.[15]

He took issue with much of what Mac Erlean had produced:

The translation of poetry from one language into another is possible provided the translator knows both languages and is a poet. All languages are equal. All languages give us access to reality. But whereas language in the raw is a pick-axe, a refinement of it, poetry, is a scalpel … Many translators say 'impossible' when they mean 'I am lazy'.[16]

The Gallery Press eventually published Hartnett's translations in 1986, to positive reviews. John F. Deane praised his version:

Hartnett succeeds in giving a 'voice' to Ó Bruadair, one of the most difficult poets in Irish, this quintessentially Gaelic poet of the seventeenth century, is direct, sometimes harsh, filled with sadness, yet always haughty and sure. Hartnett's success is in technical as well as translating the man's spirit to our times. The book is exemplary, proof that translations work when the empathy is there.[17]

Conleth Ellis in *Books Ireland* also welcomed Hartnett's work:

It would be naive to claim that Michael Hartnett's long-awaited translations from Ó Bruadair are in any way 'definitive', and I am sure this is not a claim he would himself make. Any translator's approach and technique and language are products of his own time, and there is no predicting how translators of a future generation might deal with the same material. Yet it will be difficult for them to stop their ears to the voice Hartnett has here created for Ó Bruadair, a voice that is often a delight and a triumph and always memorable.

In the inevitable comparison with Thomas Kinsella, Hartnett invariably comes out on top. He is closer to the spirit of Ó Bruadair, besides catching the tone more truly and being more faithful to the verbal music and the linguistic acrobatics. And he adds the spice of half-rhyme and vowel chiming where Kinsella is satisfied with less of the essential pyrotechnics ... For example, the last line of the poem in which Ó Bruadair lacerates the landlady who refused him a drink ... This is rendered by Kinsella as 'May she drop her dung down stupidly into the porridge!' and by Hartnett as 'like a fool in her gruel may she dribble her shit.' Hartnett scores with his onomatopoeic assonance and in the way he captures the stinginess ...[18]

Dennis O'Driscoll described Hartnett as '... in his corduroy jacket phase at the time, the sideburns long, the cigarette smoke thick, the shirt collar open, the cap flat, the manner quiet and almost courtly ...' O'Driscoll interviewed him at length in 1986, and put it to him that his 'writing sounds very much a voyage of self-discovery'. Hartnett replied:

It is all the time, yes. I'm basically a poet who has a way with words. I refuse to accept that there should be any basic intellectual or philosophic background. I deliberately try to avoid allusions in poetry to any other man's or woman's philosophy.[19]

He explained to Victoria White that 'I'm a wild horse, I must harness myself', explaining his adherence to strict verse patterns such as the sonnet: 'Verse can run away with you, but I harness it, I strap it in.'[20]

20

'A River of Tears'

As Eamon Grennan put it, 'the history of Hartnett's publications … is a bit of a jumble'.[1] Even the publisher of Hartnett's *Selected and New Poems* had to concede that it was a 'notoriously complicated publishing history'. The Dolmen Press published *Anatomy of a Cliché*, New Writers' Press published the next three books, *Hag of Beare*, *Selected Poems* and *Tao*, Goldsmith Press published *Gypsy Ballads* and *The Retreat of Ita Cagney/Cúlú Íde*, The Gallery Press published *A Farewell to English*, Raven Arts Press published *Inchicore Haiku*, and Coiscéim published some of the Irish language collections, to name but a few.

Dermot Bolger of Raven Arts Press described an early encounter with Hartnett:

> I wound up sitting in a pub off the South Circular Road between Michael and Michael Smith who had published that earlier *Selected Poems*. Both Michaels became emphatic that not only should I re-issue the long out-of-print *Selected Poems*, but that the new volume should include every poem he had written up to and including his 'Farewell to English'. Michael assured me not to worry about any copyright issues, he would take care of that.

The Gallery Press, which had published *A Farewell to English*, actually had the rights to reprint it at the time, but Bolger:

was young and naive, but even in my innocence I should have been slightly worried when he explained how he had cleared copyright permission for his wonderful translations of Lorca's 'Gypsy Ballads'. He said that he once phoned Lorca's brother in New York, explained how he had been deported from Franco's Spain and after he had read aloud a few verses the voice at the other end said: 'Spread the word brother'.[2]

This tangled publishing history probably did not help Hartnett's standing as a poet, nor perhaps did it provide him with a steady income. Moving from publisher to publisher and re-issuing different combinations of his poems hardly served his career well.

Dennis O'Driscoll once asked Hartnett, 'How important to you is recognition beyond Ireland?'

Hartnett replied:

Our sense of 'abroad' in Ireland is Britain. For years, we have been up against the great bulwark of England between us and Europe. I've been translated into Swedish, Italian, Hungarian and Spanish. But I have never been translated into English, if you know what I mean, but that isn't important to me.[3]

Hartnett's financial situation had worsened over the years. He had borrowed money in an attempt to keep going and, in fact, tried to sell the copyright of some of his poems to The Gallery Press. Peter Fallon wrote to him in August 1988:

I have been thinking about your proposal to sell us the copyright outright in respect of your work which we've published. I appreciate your needs and, obviously, I should like to be able to help. I wonder, however, exactly what you think you can offer and, generally, what kind of sum you have in mind … I wonder, however, if it's not more in your interests to discuss advances on forthcoming projects …[4]

Such were his problems at the time that Hartnett offered Dermot Bolger of Raven Arts Press a similar deal. He received a similar response:

It has taken me so long to reply to you that I am almost ashamed to write now … On the one hand I wanted to help out if at all possible and on the other I would simply never buy the copyright of another poet … I have long felt that a poet's poems are his or her own … His poems can never belong to anyone else and they are the birthright of his children and grandchildren for fifty years after his death.[5]

At the same time, in 1988, he was also attempting to sell his unpublished papers which were still in a trunk in Templeglantine. Rosemary, his estranged wife, despite the financial difficulties they were in at the time, told him he was selling himself short.

However the sum mentioned, £5,000, seems a paltry amount for your life's work. It is worth far more and you shouldn't sell yourself short because you are in a hurry to raise cash … we wouldn't want you to sacrifice it for so little. Better give what you can … Ultimately, of course, it's your decision but you'll probably get a much better offer later on.[6]

Ultimately, Hartnett returned to The Gallery Press fold. Bolger let him go: 'Naturally I'm a bit disappointed that you want to break the contract and not have the new book appear … what you really want, I think, is for all rights to the poems to revert back to you …'[7]

If the relationship of a writer and a publisher can be said to be akin to a marriage, then while Hartnett might have strayed and dallied with others over the years, in the end he returned to The Gallery Press.

At times Hartnett gave the impression that he would prefer to have lived in other times when poets had more status in society. As he told Victoria White in an *Irish Times* interview, he wished that he could have patrons like the bards of old did:

> I turn up at people's doors and say: 'My name is Michael Hartnett, I am a poet, let me in'. So far so good … They were the last defenders of Gaelic culture, and when Cromwell came, they were shocked because they were so used to getting free dinners.[8]

'Was he horrified to see what we'd lost when you started to study these poets?' Victoria White asked him.

'What struck me,' he answered, 'is what I'd lost, my dear.'[9]

Hartnett always denied that narrow nationalism was a motivation but, nevertheless, he had a strong awareness of his Irishness.

> It's just that English doesn't belong to us. I don't want to sound chauvinistic but I feel very Irish. I am Irish. I don't want to be anything else. I am aware of being a Catholic, Irish, Gaelic-speaker … I stand for a tradition … The fact that it's called Catholic is not my fault, I'm stuck with it. I'm not orthodox, I'm just myself. I drink too much. I smoke too much and I'm living with my partner.[10]

Over the years Hartnett had modified his views on Catholicism. He had told Dennis O'Driscoll, 'I was never a Catholic … I went to a lay secondary school. I was fortunate to be born in a house where my father was not a Catholic.'[11] Now he contributed to *The*

Living Word on RTÉ radio, '... having regained some of my faith by seeing the faith in others, by realising again that love and belief are possible, even to the loneliest soul, that even the most arrogant are capable of being content, capable of rediscovering humility'.[12] He recalled observing other people at prayer in church. 'I watch them with wonder, with regret, with envy ... all their sins of spite and jealousy, those great Irish faults, purged away by faith, by belief.'

He had always been impressed by the ritualistic aspect of Catholicism, in particular the old Latin masses which he remembered from his childhood in Newcastle West. 'Why do I miss Latin so much? The mass is a religious ceremony and I believe that every religious ceremony should have an element of secrecy.'[13] But he still did not have belief: 'Like a child lost at a hurling match, I can hear the applause, but cannot see the game – only a forest of overcoats.'[14] And as he put it in one of his poems: 'I tried to talk to the Creator/but the stars spat into my eyes'.

'Christianity today seems like a ruined abbey – despite its gorgeous trappings and its music: there seems to be an emptiness at its core.'[15] Despite his lack of belief, he translated the poems of Saint John of the Cross into Irish and, in 1991, Coiscéim published them.

Hartnett's heavy drinking was by then taking a toll on his health. Together with his financial problems, it contributed to his depression. In 1991, Hartnett turned fifty. He wrote a short verse for his children to mark the occasion:

Oh my darlings, oh my dears,
I have lived for fifty years;
and my hair is a river of tears –
oh my darlings, oh my dears.[16]

21

'HEARTBREAK IN TWO LANGUAGES'

In an interview, Hartnett told Victoria White, 'I happen to think in two languages. I wake up at night thinking in two languages. It breaks my heart.'[1] And now he was working in both Irish and English. Translating Gaelic poetry into English was perhaps a necessary compromise for him. In a wide-ranging interview Dennis O'Driscoll asked Hartnett how he decided which language to write in:

> Now that you are essentially a bilingual poet, is there any way in which you can tell in advance whether an idea for a poem will find expression in Irish or English?

> No, I can't tell. I've got over the notion of having intellectual schizophrenia about it. There was a period, especially in the beginning, when one line would come out in English and the next in Irish. 'The Retreat of Ita Cagney', for example, almost broke my heart and indeed my mind to write, because both languages became so intermeshed. One is not a translation of the other. They are two versions of the one poem; but what the original language is I don't know. Translating helped me enormously to come to terms with both languages.[2]

At the same time he was determined to resist easy categorisation.

As O'Driscoll described it, Hartnett was not a fan of the interview process. He was 'like a patient awaiting a medical probe, resigned to his fate but not pretending to be enamoured by it', and told O'Driscoll:

> I always lie at interviews. I don't lie as such but I change my mind so often. I refuse to have what is known in the trade as a 'coherent metaphysic' … I've been trying to pin myself down … but I couldn't do it – neither am I a butterfly nor is my other self a lepidopterist.[3]

Peter Fallon, his publisher, detected a lack of confidence in Hartnett with regard to his poetry in the Irish language: 'I believe he lost faith in his own Irish following his "return" to English.'[4] Michael Smith believed that when Hartnett's 'own lyrical gift began to fail … Michael turned to translations from the Irish, translation always being a good means of keeping one's skills honed.'[5]

In a sense, the translations were his way of staying in touch with his Gaelic spirit. As Eamon Grennan suggested, Hartnett had embarked on:

> a journey that starts, stops, starts again, doubles back on itself, pursues false paths, tries different approaches, feels its way into the clear, and presses deliberately and forcefully ahead. There is progress but the way it is achieved suggests more a man in a maze.[6]

Hartnett did not revere the Gaelic poets for their own sake.

> Because of the military and social impositions placed on this country from time to time by an alien power we tend to look back in astonishment at the fact our poets and language survived rather than

calmly assess the literary value of their poetry: we do not have poets, we have salvagers and therefore the dangerous corollary arises that anything that is salvaged is good.[7]

He aspired to the social influence that these Gaelic poets had in their time. As Seamus Heaney asserted, 'Maybe "prophet" is too strong a word to apply to Michael Hartnett, although from beginning to end he was not shy of embracing the role of representative bard.'[8] Theo Dorgan believed that Hartnett was a 'profound democrat, in that he identified always with the poor and marginalised, he was an aristocrat in spirit, and carried himself with the air of a man whose hand was never far from the hilt of a Spanish sword'.[9]

Yet there was a certain inconsistency at the heart of Hartnett's translations when he turned away from the modernism of much of his early poetry to look towards his country's past. Thomas O'Grady saw the apparent contradiction: 'At once an iconoclast and a throwback, Hartnett aspired to realise the not-quite-paradox of both breaking with convention and embracing tradition.'[10] But Hartnett felt that every generation should produce their own translation. He was quite prepared to be outmoded: 'I hope it shall be done again by someone else in twenty or thirty years: sufficient unto the generation is the translator thereof.'[11] Hartnett was of the opinion that some poets had other reasons to take it up:

There is another form of translation – imitation – which is a much inferior exercise: it is a sure way of producing minor interesting verse and is generally practised when a poet hits a barren period, or worse, by poets who are technically able but short on themes.[12]

Hartnett felt that his translations were not appreciated. In his introduction to the poems of Father Pádraigín Haicéad, a Dominican priest who had spent much of his life in exile, he wrote:

> I have not, of course, caught the beauty of his Irish. Some of the close-lipped Irish speaking writers of today do not approve of translations from the language, it is as if they do not want to share poets they do not read themselves … I hope that readers of this book will not be led away but towards the real Haicéad.[13]

Douglas Sealy was impressed by Hartnett's ability to work his way through 'the stylistic thicket of his [Haicéad's] Irish'.[14]

In many ways, this was Hartnett's compromise solution; he would translate Gaelic poets into modern vernacular English, and the poets he chose had a resonance for him as they were Munster poets from his home area and, like him, were outsiders in the society in which they had lived. In his translations of Haicéad, Ó Bruadair and Ó Rathaille, Hartnett:

> found voices in the Munster tradition which operated as an extension of his private voice of disenchantment with the transformations of modern Ireland … This work involved a formidable enterprise in Gaelic scholarship, but it gave him access to an idiom echoing his own; the metres were complex and, for the translator, sometimes intractable, but the idiom was rich, and had a fertile vein of rancour which was just the right instrument.[15]

Hartnett could be very sensitive to any negative commentary in public on his poetry, particularly if it came from those he regarded as friends. Gabriel Rosenstock recounts one such event: 'I criticised his Ó Rathaille translations in *Poetry Ireland Review.*

I'm told he took it badly. I took it badly that he took it badly. There's something about Ireland that makes criticism impossible.'[16] Rosenstock had been quite acerbic so perhaps he should have been less surprised:

> Frank O'Connor's translations have a more seductive melody than Hartnett's, for this reader at any rate, and in Ó Rathaille it's the breathtaking sweep and majesty of the music, the powerful orchestration, that creates the vitriol, the chagrin, the high tragedy ... I feel we're moving perilously towards William McGonigle territory ... The bathos found in some of these translations merely attests to the fact that Irish and English are worlds apart; the English, here, is often pulseless and lacks the linguistic accrescences of the original ... Hartnett's Introduction is skimpy. Ó Rathaille needs to be placed in the socio-political context of the seventeenth and eighteenth century and we need a key to understand his literary and linguistic conventions, as well as a handful of allusions ... Ó Rathaille's satires – and Hartnett has a well-known penchant for such material – remind us all how tame and politically correct we have become. But much of the minor poetry in this volume reads like doggerel. In fairness, I think I have indicated sufficiently that one was attempting the impossible here and there's no substituting the original article.[17]

Desmond Traynor in *Books Ireland* was more positive:

> My inadequacies when reviewing this volume of Michael Hartnett's translations from the seventeenth- and eighteenth-century Irish of Aodhaghán Ó Rathaille are manifest and manifold, woefully under-qualified as I am in the native tongue. Perhaps a Gaelic scholar or folklorist will write more comprehensively about Hartnett's skills as a translator in a future issue of this magazine. In the meantime, all I can offer is the view that Hartnett's English versions of the aislings

and elegies, political and satirical poems of this great Gaelic poet have all the delicacy and finesse we associate with much of his own poetry in English … while at the same time capturing a sense of the capacious energy available in the original metres, and giving a flavour of the rambunctious colloquial speech of the language of the originals. They are ultimately very sad, chronicling as they do personal demise, as well as that of an entire civilisation.[18]

Hartnett was essentially writing his translations for people like Desmond Traynor, who did not have the Irish to read these poems in their original language. It was a far cry from his original intention when he announced his farewell to English. Máire Mhac an tSaoi was of the opinion that:

Michael Hartnett for many years followed a self-denying ordinance and wrote in Irish; it did not work. His understanding of Irish was profound, but the magic inhered in his English. Now his English translations of seventeenth- and eighteenth-century Gaelic poets read like original productions, instinct with what I can only describe as tough-minded Irishness.[19]

She believed that Hartnett used his Irish poetry to kick-start his English writing.

Hartnett, we must place in a class alone. That his work in Irish has undoubtedly enormously enriched his muse in English is undisputed, so is his eminent status as a poet, and yet I think that for him the importance of the Irish must always be that it primes the pump for his English.[20]

One suspects that this was a view not shared by Hartnett himself.

22

'ALCOHOL'S A CUNNING BEAST'

Hartnett had always been a drinker but as time went on he drank more and more. It was not that he was unaware of its power over him:

> Alcohol's a cunning beast.
> It fools the doctor and the priest,
> it fools the clever and the sane –
> but not the liver or the brain.[1]

Younger poet Tony Curtis saw firsthand the effect that the drink had:

> To some people it often looked as if Michael had his hand firmly over the self-destruct button – maybe some days he had – but when I used say to him that drink would be the death of him, he'd reply 'I've no wish to die'. But still he went on drinking, believing it a necessary part of his creativity.[2]

His friends were concerned. John B. Keane replied to a long-delayed letter from Hartnett: 'A blessing in itself to hear from you. I always had a worry you'd vanish some day into a hissing shower or summer haze in spite of yourself.'[3] Paul Durcan held a similar view:

I believe that being the ruthlessly logical artist that he was, he cal-
culated that in order to survive as a poet in Dublin city he would be
compelled to drink hard liquor in extreme and regular quantities. I
believe he made a secret pact with himself in the privacy of his soul.
Knowing full well that the price would be an early death but believing that it was the only method of living whereby he would be able
to continue writing poetry ...[4]

Hartnett could analyse the stages he went through when he
drank. At first, he would be jolly, optimistic, very garrulous. 'Then
I snap, like my father ... alcohol becomes part of you, part of your
system.'[5]

Durcan took issue with the public image of Hartnett. He
saw him as 'sophisticated, iconoclastic, analytical, encyclopaedic,
cosmopolitan, droll, ironic, tragicomic', and not 'the doomed
hobgoblin of the literary world'.[6] Tony Curtis noted Hartnett's
driven nature:

He had the extraordinary trait of all great poets, a total belief in his
gift and a terror that it might desert him: there would be no peace,
inside or outside poetry. After all it is not something you can practise
or polish, it is a curse and a pure blessing.[7]

As he aged it perhaps became more of a burden. He told Victoria
White of *The Irish Times*, 'It's frightening starting again, I wake
up every morning saying – "It's all finished"'.

Dennis O'Driscoll asked about his prolific nature: 'Do you try
to set aside a space in every day for writing?'

'No, I can't. I have blank periods which last anything from 6
months to 2 years.'[8]

But, at the same time, he felt that he must continue his

struggle, 'I feel I'm passing something on. I feel it is my duty … I belong to the Gaelic poets and they to me.'[9]

Hartnett was conscious that he was getting older:

> I am aware that every literary generation matures into begrudgery; the attitude shared by many poets in their fifties seems to be one of finality. All the better poets are dead or dying, they believe: they see no promise in the young, they pull down the blinds and potter in rooms of the past.[10]

Hartnett liked the convivial nature of pub culture. Christine Dwyer Hickey saw this first hand, on an eventful trip to a literary festival.

> Every pub, no matter where it was became his local the minute he entered the premises. The barman would invariably know him, the owner would usually come out for a word, the oul lad in the corner would put down his paper, the lush hiding in the snug would suddenly emerge.[11]

Over the years, Hartnett had been very active promoting his own work by appearing at poetry readings. But in later years Nuala Ní Dhomhnaill noticed a change in his attitude: 'he was going through a stage where he seemed to hate his audience'.[12]

Aosdána (from *aos dána*, 'people of the arts') is an Irish association of artists, which was created in 1981 with support from the Arts Council of Ireland. Both Hartnett and Ní Dhomhnaill were elected to Aosdána and often made common cause on the committee. As she described him, Hartnett had 'those wonderful dark eyes that were in his case very much the windows of the soul. These eyes could gleam with fun and malice and quick, mischievous glee.'[13]

For five years Hartnett was the beneficiary of a *Cnuas*, an annuity of £5,000 that members of Aosdána, resident in Ireland, were eligible to receive from the Arts Council to enable them to concentrate their time and energies in the full-time pursuit of their art. Hartnett translated some of Ní Dhomhnaill's poems into English for a Raven Arts publication. According to her, 'At the subsequent book-launch Michael took one look at my thunderstruck face when I discovered that the Irish originals had not been included and said to Angela Liston, his companion, that they had better skedaddle.'[14]

Now that he was living again in the Baggot Street area Hartnett frequented Parson's Bookshop. Mary King from the shop kept an anxious eye on him. 'Near-neighbour Michael Hartnett, who with his cap looked like a jockey out of a Jack Yeats or Harry Kernoff picture. We all hoped that Michael would give up the drink.'[15]

'The stuff will kill me,' he told her one day.

On one occasion, Dermot Bolger was waiting for an overdue manuscript from Hartnett, who eventually turned up. 'He handed me the proofs … and ever the optimist, asked if by any chance I might have the loan of £5,000 … I bought him lunch instead …'[16] Afterwards, Bolger accompanied Hartnett to some films in the Irish Film Centre to see Francis Ford Coppola's *Rumblefish*, 'shot entirely in moody black and white. The only object filmed in colour was one solitary fighting fish in a glass tank.' At the end of the film Bolger commented on that cinematic trick. Hartnett gripped his arm and with the relief of a man who had known the delusional tricks of delirium tremens whispered, 'Oh, thank God, you saw the fish too.'[17]

He was hospitalised on a number of occasions. His diary for April 1989 had the laconic note, 'Clane Hospital 7th April–24th

April 1989 cirrhosis of liver ... will live ...'[18] His time in Room 8 was commemorated in a poem:

> Indoors, the seasons change no coat or fashion.
> Ladies, white and blue, appear and disappear,
> dispensing comfort care, compassion.
> When I confuse despair with ordinary fear
> and the fabric of my soul starts to unravel
> I head for Clane ...[19]

Although Hartnett had periods when he dried out and sobered up, often entailing stays in hospital, his drinking damaged his relationship with his two teenage children, who visited him and his partner Angela Liston in Dublin occasionally.

Nuala Ní Dhomhnaill remembered Hartnett at this stage as still 'beautifully and formally dressed in a brown-hued tweed suit but never very large, severely wasting away to nothing'.[20]

Hartnett's lifestyle was increasingly pub-centred. Michael Smith recalled how, 'after Hartnett's early-evening court sessions in Doheny and Nesbitt's, his admirers (often cultivated and literary civil servants) would head off to their respectable homes in the suburbs, leaving Michael as an abandoned court jester.'[21]

Brighid McLaughlin of the *Sunday Independent* had some memorable encounters with Hartnett. One interview began at 10:30 in the morning in the Leeson Lounge, where the clientele were watching the FTSE Index on Sky News. Hartnett formally introduced them all to her one-by-one: 'Four millionaires, a broken poet and a journalist,' said Michael.[22] 'For a small man he is loved hugely. His favourite role as the awful rogue, the terrible liar, has its own disarming charm, but it is his status as a "real poet" that has gained so much admiration.' McLaughlin felt that

Hartnett 'drifted through Dublin like a ship with no fuel to get him moving and no anchor to keep him in one place'.[23]

'I'm big in Finland,' he once told her.

In fact, he was a fan of Finnish composer Sibelius. In some ways he identified with him; another man beset with alcoholic tendencies. As fellow poet and friend Pat O'Brien put it, 'Michael loved music and some of his great later poems would engage with Mozart and Sibelius but the tin whistle was closest to his own voice, its airs "the flight of birds", its notes "wings of parchment".'[24]

Paul Durcan understood that Hartnett was 'a lover of music of all kinds ranging from Elvis Presley and Buddy Holly to Irish traditional music to Mozart, Tchaikovsky, Schumann and, above all, Sibelius'.[25] And, according to Durcan, Hartnett had another reason for identifying so strongly with Sibelius, who was 'born a Swedish-speaking Finn in a Finland tyrannised by Tsarist Russia, who did not begin to learn and speak Finnish until the age of eight'.[26]

Fred Johnston, who encountered Hartnett on several occasions in his later life, saw him as an outsider. To him, Hartnett:

had a bird-like nervous energy caged in by a drinker's fatalism; he could be powerful and defiant and upsetting and impossible. I think he scared off the more pietistic birds in our Irish poets' aviary and the result was a very Irish kind of half-reverence: while admiring his work, voices were lowered when a reading was suggested.[27]

Johnston saw this as a form of hypocrisy:

While praising Hartnett and needing him as the rambunctious heir to a capricious and disinherited Gaelic bardic order, there were those, poets and administrators alike, who shied away from his mis-

chievous physical presence, wishing him respectable … But Hartnett was a song-bird with his own song, while too many of the rest
were simply mynah birds aping someone else's whistle. He upset the
drawing-room avariciousness of the New Irish Poetry. Hartnett's
like will not be seen again. The New Irish Poetry will not allow it.
It's uncomfortable to say that Hartnett was marginalised, but he
was, his shifts in and out of Irish observed as one might observe the
frivolities of a strange exotic bird. Besides, the New Irish Poetry is
about grants, readings, ascension into Aosdána and, in some cases,
acquiring fashionable hats and accents; it's certainly not about any
sort of Gaelic tradition or bardic upkeep … Hartnett knew how
much we believed in him and to what extent we thought him an
unfortunate clown. We could be appallingly patronising to him. The
New Irish Poetry whose sense of tradition is often unreckonable,
struggled with him. I and, I'm sure, not a few others, would have
given an arm and a leg to possess the creative word-magic Hartnett
inherited.[28]

Over the years Hartnett's decline was noticeable to his friends.
Though he was still dressed as neatly as before, his physical decline was palpable. Nuala Ní Dhomhnaill was shocked at his
appearance when she encountered him in 1999: 'He was drunk.
Unusually enough for me, I took him aside and said I thought he
was doing harm to his health. "Nuala," he said, "what does it matter? My work is done".'[29]

Hartnett was in discussion with The Gallery Press with a view
to publishing an edition of his *Collected Poems*. As he had written
himself in a review years before:

There is something very final in the words 'Collected Poems'. Here,
the total poet, if not the total man, is held up for examination. In the
case of a dead poet nothing can be added, nothing taken away. His

reputation stands on the few pages into which his whole life should have gone.[30]

When drinking, he didn't take care of himself. Tony Curtis noted, 'While I couldn't say he loved eating, he did love cooking.'[31] According to James Liddy, Hartnett told Nuala Ní Dhomhnaill that he blamed his ill health on 'Natasha'.

'Natasha who?' she asked.

'Natasha Smirnoff.'[32]

The more he drank the more likely he was to fly into a rage. Dermot Bolger recalled one occasion:

> In Conway's Pub somebody said something that annoyed him. He swept past me, making for the door, the coat swinging … At the door he turned to brandish his stick in the air and disappeared into the night, looking like a ghost from an eighteenth-century poem.[33]

Michael Hartnett became ill during Listowel Writers' Week and suffered convulsions in the local hospital. He was transferred to St Vincent's Hospital, Dublin, where he died on 13 October 1999. He was fifty-eight years old.

Conclusion

As Seamus Heaney remarked:

> Michael Hartnett's inspirations affected Irish poetry the way a power surge affects the grid: things quickened and shone when he published. Yet, in spite of that, his achievement was undernoticed. Slight of build and disinclined to flaunt himself on the literary scene, he was always more focused on his creative journey than on career moves.[1]

Eamon Grennan also invoked the image of a man on a voyage of exploration:

> For the trajectory made by Hartnett's work ... is not a neat uninterrupted arc. It is more like a journey that starts, stops, starts again, doubles back on itself, pursues false paths, tries different approaches, feels its way into the clear, then presses deliberately and forcefully ahead. The poet, that is, doesn't proceed easily along the open road; certainly there is progress ... but the way it is achieved suggests more a man moving about in a maze.[2]

In 1974, Hartnett's decision to no longer write in English may have been a drastic act of artistic self-denial but it showed his commitment to the Irish language, which he had first learned on his grandmother's farm.

Hartnett's return to writing in English was perhaps inevitable, and should be seen not as a defeat but as a compromise. For the rest of his life he wrote mainly in English, but he used his knowledge of Irish to translate the poems of Ó Bruadair, Ó Rathaille and Haicéad for a modern audience. Hartnett identified with these Gaelic poets, in particular with their estrangement from the society in which they lived, which mirrored his own alienation from modern Ireland.

Hartnett remained in thrall to the language he felt he had never quite mastered. In the documentary, *A Necklace of Wrens*, filmed in the year of his death he confessed: 'My attitude towards the Irish language is one of dismay and great love, dismay because I don't do it enough justice.'[3]

In his own words:

Poets with progress
make no peace or pact:
the act of poetry
is a rebel act.[4]

Michael Hartnett devoted his life to his rebel act.

ENDNOTES

INTRODUCTION

1 Hartnett, M., 'Why Write in Irish?', *The Irish Times* (26 August 1975), p. 8.
2 'Poet on the Move', *The Kerryman* (25 July 1975), p. 7.
3 White, V., 'Heartbreak in Two Languages', *The Irish Times* (15 December 1994).
4 Hartnett, 'Why Write in Irish?', p. 8.
5 Gillespie, E., 'Michael Hartnett', *The Irish Times* (5 March 1975), p. 10.
6 Hartnett, M., *A Farewell to English* (Dublin, The Gallery Press, 1975), p. 33.
7 *Ibid.*, p. 32.
8 *Ibid.*, p. 34.
9 *Ibid.*, p. 33.
10 *Ibid.*, p. 35.

1. '1941 WAS A TERRIBLE YEAR'

1 Hartnett, M., 'Maiden Street Ballad', *A Book of Strays* (Oldcastle, The Gallery Press, 2002), p. 28.
2 *Ibid.*
3 McDonagh, J. and Newman, S., *Remembering Michael Hartnett* (Dublin, Four Courts Press, 2006), p. 16.
4 *A Necklace of Wrens* [Film], Harvest Films, 1999.
5 Ní Dhomhnaill, N., 'Foighne Crainn: The Patience of a Tree'; *Metre*, 11 (2001), p. 148.
6 Hartnett, 'Why Write in Irish?', p. 8.
7 *A Necklace of Wrens.*
8 *Ibid.*
9 Hartnett, M., 'The Town the Young leave', *The Irish Times* (10 June 1969), p. 11.
10 Hartnett, M., 'A Small Farm', *Collected Poems* (Oldcastle, The Gallery Press, 2001), p. 15.
11 *A Necklace of Wrens.*
12 O'Driscoll, D., Interview, *Metre*, 11 (2001), p. 142.

13 Hartnett, 'The Town the Young leave', p. 11.

14 *A Necklace of Wrens*.

15 Curtis, T., 'A Life in Poetry', *Metre*, 11 (2001), p. 166.

16 Hartnett, 'The Town the Young leave', p. 11.

17 *Ibid.*

18 Hartnett, M., 'Notes on "Maiden Street Ballad"', *A Book of Strays*, p. 60.

19 *Ibid.*, p. 64.

20 Hartnett, 'The Town the Young leave', p. 11.

21 Hartnett, *A Book of Strays*, p. 41.

22 *Ibid.*

23 *Ibid.*, p. 63.

24 Hartnett, M., papers, National Library 35,910/4.

25 Hartnett, M., 'Christmas in Newcastle West', *Old Limerick Journal*, 17 (Winter 1984), p. 16.

26 *A Necklace of Wrens*.

27 Hartnett, 'The Town the Young leave', p. 11.

28 Hartnett, M., cited in Clarke, R. D., *Austin Clarke remembered* (1996), p. 46.

29 Hartnett, *A Book of Strays*, p. 63.

30 Hartnett, 'Christmas in Newcastle West', p. 16.

31 *Ibid.*

32 *Ibid.*

33 Hartnett, 'The Town the Young leave', p. 11.

34 *Ibid.*

35 *Ibid.*

36 Hartnett, 'Christmas in Newcastle West', p. 16.

37 *A Necklace of Wrens*.

38 Hartnett, 'Why Write in Irish?', p. 8.

2. 'LOOK WHAT HE WROTE FOR ME'

1 Hartnett, M., 'Wrestling with Ó Bruadair', in MacReamoinn, S., *The Pleasures of Gaelic Poetry* (London, Allen Lane, 1982), p. 65.

2 Hartnett, M., 'Poet's Progress', *The Irish Times* (11 November 1968), p. 6.

3 *Ibid.*

4 Hartnett, 'The Town the Young leave', p. 11.

5 *Ibid.*

6 Hartnett, 'Poet's Progress', p. 6.

7 *A Necklace of Wrens*.

8 Clarke, *Austin Clarke remembered*, p. 46.

9 *Ibid.*

10 Hartnett, 'Poet's Progress', p. 6.

11 Hartnett, *A Book of Strays*, p. 28.

12 Hartnett, 'The Town the Young leave', p. 11.

13 *Ibid.*

14 Hartnett, M., papers, National Library 35,942.

15 Hartnett, M., 'The Lord Taketh Away', *Collected Poems* (Oldcastle, The Gallery Press, 2001), p. 48.

16 Hartnett, M., papers, National Library 35,910/3.

17 Hartnett, M., 'Radio', *Hibernia* (17 January 1977), p. 35.

18 Durcan, P., 'The Achievement of Michael Hartnett', *The Cork Examiner* (27 February 1978), p. 5.

19 Hartnett, 'Poet's Progress', p. 6.

20 Hartnett, M., *The Irish Times* (9 June 1969), p. 11.

21 Hartnett, *A Book of Strays*, pp. 62f.

3. 'THE EMIGRANT STINT'

1 Hartnett, M., 'London and the Emigrant Stint', *The Irish Times* (12 November 1968), p. 6.

2 *Ibid.*

3 *Ibid.*

4 *Ibid.*

5 *Ibid.*

6 *Ibid.*

7 Hartnett, 'Why Write in Irish?', p. 8.

8 O'Riordan, D., *The Irish Times* (31 March 1969), p. 10.

9 Jordan, J., Review, *Cyphers*, 11 (Winter 1979), p. 45.

10 Hartnett, M., Letter, John Jordan papers, National Library 35,077.

11 *Ibid.*

12 Hartnett, 'Short Mass', *Collected Poems* (2001), p. 21.

13 Lisker, R., 'Poetry and Literary Pubs', *Hibernia* (24 October 1969), p. 22.

14 Hartnett, 'Her Diadem, Pain …', *Collected Poems* (2001), p. 29.

4. 'YOU INSOLENT PUP'

1 Foley, D., 'Tea-boy of the Western World', *Sunday Review* (23 July 1961), p. 4.

2 *Ibid.*

3 *Ibid.*

4 Hartnett, 'Poet's Progress', p. 6.

5   McLaughlin, B., 'The Terrier Poet at Home on the Hillside', *The Irish Press* (28 September 1978), p. 9.
6   Hartnett, 'Poet's Progress', p. 6.
7   *Ibid.*
8   *Ibid.*
9   Jordan, J., papers, National Library 35,041/2 (1–28).
10 *Ibid.*
11 Hartnett, 'Sickroom', *Collected Poems* (2001), p. 16.
12 Hartnett, 'Sulphur', *Collected Poems* (2001), p. 20.
13 Hartnett, 'Poet's Progress', p. 6.
14 *Ibid.*
15 Hartnett, M., 'The Dublin Literary World', *The Irish Times* (13 November 1968), p. 6.
16 Liddy, J., *The Doctor's House* (Clare, Salmon Publishing, 2004), p. 82.
17 *Ibid.*, pp. 82f.
18 Hartnett, 'Poet's Progress', p. 6.
19 *Ibid.*
20 Smith, M., 'Remembering Michael Hartnett', *The Irish Times* (16 February 2009).
21 Smith, M., 'Closed Circuit', *The Irish Times* (2 April 1971), p. 10.
22 O'Driscoll, Interview, p. 144.
23 Hartnett, 'The Poet Down', *Collected Poems* (2001), p. 93.
24 Hartnett, M., 'Radio', *Hibernia* (29 April 1977), p. 29.
25 'From Limerick who writes and writes', *Sunday Independent* (16 September 1962), p. 18.

5. 'I FAILED *CUM LAUDE*'

1   Jordan, J., Editorial, *Poetry Ireland*, 1, 1 (1962), p. 3.
2   Jordan, J., papers, National Library 35,077.
3   *Ibid.*
4   *Ibid.*, 35,089.
5   Bardwell, L., *A Restless Life* (Dublin, Liberties Press, 2008), p. 261.
6   Liddy, *The Doctor's House*, p. 82.
7   *Ibid.*, p. 84.
8   *Ibid.*, p. 83.
9   *Ibid.*
10 Hartnett, 'The Dublin Literary World', p. 6.
11 McFadden, H., *Crystal Clear: The Selected Prose of John Jordan* (Dublin, Lilliput Press, 2006), p. 3.

12 Liddy, J., Letter dated 26 February 1963, New Writers' Press Records, National Library Manuscripts 40,136/1.

13 Smith, M., 'John Jordan: Beyond Categories …', *The Irish Times* (14 June 1988), p. 12.

14 Smith, 'Closed Circuit', p. 10.

15 Kilroy, T., 'In memoriam: John Jordan', *Irish Review*, 6 (Spring 1989), p. 95.

16 Liddy, *The Doctor's House*, p. 82.

17 Liddy, J., *The Full Shilling* (Clare, Salmon Publishing, 2009), p. 98.

18 Smith, 'Remembering Michael Hartnett'.

19 *Ibid.*

20 Liddy, *The Doctor's House*, p. 82.

21 Smith, M., 'Michael Hartnett: A Memoir', *Metre*, 11 (2001), p. 156.

22 Smith, 'Closed Circuit', p. 10.

23 Grennan, E., *Facing the Music: Irish Poetry in the Twentieth Century* (Omaha, Creighton University Press, 1999), p. 296.

24 *Ibid.*, p. 297.

25 Woods, M., 'Ten Years of Irish poetry', *Hibernia* (17 April 1970), p. 20.

26 Grennan, *Facing the Music*, p. 297.

27 Bardwell, *A Restless Life*, pp. 255f.

28 *Ibid.*, p. 255.

29 McFadden, H., cited in Hartnett, N. (ed.), *Notes from his Contemporaries: A Tribute to Michael Hartnett* (Lulu, 2010), p. 114.

30 Clarke, *Austin Clarke remembered*, pp. 46f.

31 *Ibid.*

32 *Ibid.*, p. 47.

33 *Ibid.*, pp. 47f.

34 Liddy, *The Doctor's House*, pp. 50f.

35 Jordan, J., papers, National Library 35,077.

36 *Ibid.*

37 Hartnett, 'The Dublin Literary World', p. 6.

38 Gillespie, 'Michael Hartnett', p. 10.

39 McLaughlin, 'The Terrier Poet at Home on the Hillside', p. 9.

6. 'TRUST NOTHING YOU WRITE'

1 McFadden, H., cited in Hartnett, N., *Notes from his Contemporaries*, p. 114.

2 Liddy, J., Letter, New Writers' Press Records, National Library 40,136/1.

3 Fennell, D., 'Welcome to the *Arena*', *The Irish Press* (27 May 1963), p. 9.

4 Quidnunc, 'Irishman's Diary', *The Irish Times* (27 November 1963), p. 12.

5   Cited in Begnal, M. S. (ed.), *Honeysuckle, Honeyjuice: A Tribute to James Liddy* (Galway, Arlen House, 2006), p. 17.

6   *Ibid.*, p. 64.

7   Liddy, J., *This was Arena* (1982), p. 5.

8   Liddy, *The Doctor's House*, p. 56.

9   *Ibid.*, p. 61.

10 Liddy, *This was Arena*, p. 5.

11 Editorial, *Arena*, 3 (Summer 1964), p. 1.

12 Jordan, J., *Poetry Ireland*, 3 (Spring 1964), p. 3.

13 *Ibid.*

14 Cited in Duffy, N. and Dorgan, T. (eds), *Watching the River flow: A Century in Irish Poetry* (Dublin, *Poetry Ireland*, 1999), pp. 137f.

15 Woods, M., 'John Jordan 1930–1988', *Poetry Ireland Review*, 25 (Spring, 1989), p. 15.

16 Jordan, *Poetry Ireland*, 3, p. 3.

17 Liddy, *The Doctor's House*, p. 86.

18 Hartnett, M., 'Tao', *This was Arena* (Naas, The Malton Press, 1982), p. 42.

19 O'Driscoll, Interview, p. 145.

20 *Ibid.*

21 Hartnett, N., *Notes from his Contemporaries*, p. 115.

22 Nicholson, R., 'Signatures of all Things I am here to read', *James Joyce Quarterly*, 38, 3–4 (Spring/Summer 2001), p. 294.

23 Liddy, *The Doctor's House*, p. 48.

24 Brennan, R., Review, *Books Ireland* (September 2003), p. 200.

25 Durcan, P., 'Ulysses', in *Daddy, Daddy* (Belfast, Blackstaff Press, 1990), pp. 99–101.

26 Curtis, 'A Life in Poetry', p. 168.

27 Hartnett, M., 'Tao', *Poems in English* (Dublin, The Dolmen Press, 1977), p. 65.

28 Hartnett, N., *Notes from his Contemporaries*, p. 115.

29 Kersnowski, F., *The Outsiders: Poets of Contemporary Ireland* (Fort Worth, Texan Christian University Press, 1975), pp. 34f.

30 Editorial, *Arena*, 4 (Spring 1965), p. 1.

31 O'Driscoll, Interview, p. 142.

32 Hartnett, 'Thirteen Poems Written in Madrid', *This was Arena*, p. 106.

33 Liddy, *This was Arena*, p. 5.

34 Liddy, *The Doctor's House*, p. 85.

35 Hartnett, 'The Poet as Saint', *A Book of Strays*, p. 13.

36 Liddy, J., cited in Hartnett, N., *Notes from his Contemporaries*, p. 102.

37 Liddy, *The Doctor's House*, pp. 85f.

38 *Ibid.*, p. 86.

39 Rosemary Hartnett, correspondence with the author.

40 *Ibid.*

41 McFadden, *Crystal Clear*, p. 12.

42 Durcan, P., 'Hartnett's Farewell', in Montague, J. (ed.), *The Poet's Chair* (Dublin, Lilliput Press, 2008), p. 217.

43 *Ibid.*

44 *Ibid.*, p. 218.

45 Hartnett, 'The Dublin Literary World', p. 6.

46 Gillespie, 'Michael Hartnett', p. 10.

7. 'Golgotha, Gentlemen, please'

1 *A Necklace of Wrens* (1999).

2 Hartnett, *The Irish Times* (9 June 1969), p. 11.

3 Hartnett, 'The Town the Young leave', p. 11.

4 *Ibid.*

5 Hartnett, 'London and the Emigrant Stint', p. 6.

6 Lynch, B., Biographical notes, *The Holy Door*, 2 (Winter 1965), p. 35.

7 Rosemary Hartnett, correspondence with the author.

8 Hartnett, 'I Will Pay Court to You ...', *Collected Poems* (2001), p. 69.

9 Liddy, *The Doctor's House*, p. 83.

10 Lynch, B., Letter dated 18 December 1978, Michael Hartnett papers, National Library 35,914/8(2–3).

11 Hartnett, M., papers, National Library 35,91/4(1).

12 Liddy, J., cited in Hartnett, N., *Notes from his Contemporaries*, p. 102.

13 Hartnett, 'The Poet as Saint', *A Book of Strays*, p. 13.

14 Liddy, *The Full Shilling*, pp. 60–63.

15 *Ibid.*

16 Rosemary Hartnett, correspondence with the author.

8. 'The Zeal for Metre and Syllable'

1 'An Irishman's Diary', *The Irish Times* (3 August 1968), p. 11.

2 Gillespie, 'Michael Hartnett', p. 10.

3 Rosemary Hartnett, correspondence with the author.

4 Hartnett, 'London and the Emigrant Stint', p. 6.

5 Smith, 'Remembering Michael Hartnett', p. 12.

6 Smith, M., 'Introduction to New Irish Poets', in Joyce, T., *Sole Glum Trek*

(Dublin, New Writers' Press, 1967), pp. 5f.

7   Quidnunc, 'Irishman's Diary', *The Irish Times* (1 April 1969), p. 25.

8   *The Irish Times* (4 April 1969), p. 9.

9   Smith, M. and Joyce, T., Editorial, *The Lace Curtain*, 2 (Spring 1970), p. 2.

10 Murphy, H., 'State of the Nation', *The Irish Times* (9 July 1969), p. 9.

11 *Ibid.*

12 Rosemary Hartnett, correspondence with the author.

13 Sealy, D., 'Four Poets', *The Irish Times* (10 August 1968), p. 11.

14 Hartnett, M., Review, *Hibernia* (18 December 1970), p. 12.

15 O'Driscoll, Interview, p. 139.

16 Hartnett, 'London and the Emigrant Stint', p. 6.

17 Smith, 'Michael Hartnett: A Memoir', p. 126.

18 Joyce, T., 'New Writers' Press', in Coughlan, P. and Davies, A. (eds), *Modernism and Ireland: The Poetry of the 1930s* (Cork, Cork University Press, 1995), p. 279.

19 *Ibid.*

20 *Ibid.*, p. 288.

21 Smith, M., Letter, *The Irish Times* (29 April 1969), p. 16.

22 *Ibid.*

23 O'Driscoll, Interview, p. 140.

24 Armstrong, J., 'A new Force in Irish Poetry Publishing', *The Irish Times* (27 January 1972), p. 10.

25 Simmons, J., 'New Talent', *Fortnight*, 64 (22 June 1973), p. 18.

26 Scannell, V., 'Craft and Matter', *The Irish Press* (8 May 1971), p. 12.

27 *Ibid.*

28 Lynch, B., Letters, *The Irish Press* (13 May 1971), p. 8.

29 Boland, E., 'The Poet facing both Ways', *The Irish Times* (29 January 1971), p. 12.

30 *Ibid.*

31 Liddy, J., Letter dated 1971, National Library, New Writers' Press Records 40,136/2.

32 Joyce, 'New Writers' Press', in Coughlan and Davies, *Modernism and Ireland*, p. 279.

33 McGurk, T., 'Spring Poetry', *The Irish Times* (13 May 1972), p. 10.

34 Hartnett, M. and Ryan, R., Letters, *The Irish Times* (23 June 1972), p. 11.

35 *Ibid.*

36 Hartnett, M., Letters, *The Irish Times*, 27 June 1972, p. 11.

37 McGurk, T., Letters, *The Irish Times* (10 July 1972), p. 1.

9. 'Till, Talk and Tankard'

1   Liddy, J., 'A Poetry Reading', *Kilkenny Magazine* (Spring 1965), pp. 35–37.
2   Boland, E., 'Poetry Reading at Project Arts Centre', *The Irish Times* (2 August 1971), p. 8.
3   Murphy, 'State of the Nation', p. 9.
4   Lisker, 'Poetry and Literary Pubs', p. 22.
5   *Ibid.*
6   Smith, M., Editorial, *The Lace Curtain*, 4 (Summer 1971), pp. 3f.
7   Smith, 'Closed Circuit', p. 10.
8   McCafferty, N., 'At the Poetry Recital', *The Irish Times* (9 March 1971), p. 10.
9   O'Driscoll, Interview, p. 140.
10 Rosemary Hartnett, correspondence with the author.
11 *Ibid.*
12 Ní Fhrighil, M., Review, *The Irish Times* (13 March 1973), p. 10.
13 Boland, J., 'Poetry', *The Irish Press* (15 February 1972), p. 5.
14 'The Small Imprints', *The Irish Times* (6 November 1973), p. 10.
15 Rushe, D., 'Tatler's Parade', *Irish Independent* (2 November 1973), p. 8.

10. 'Exquisite Dream of a Poet'

1   Montague, J., *Company* (2001), p. 30.
2   Hartnett, 'Why Write in Irish?', p. 8.
3   'The Future of Irish Poetry', *The Irish Times* (5 February 1970), p. 14.
4   Hartnett, M., 'Closed Circuit', *The Irish Times* (23 April 1971), p. 12.
5   Smith, 'Closed Circuit', p. 10.
6   Lynch, B., *Parson's Bookshop* (Dublin, Liffey Press, 2006), p. 129.
7   McFadden, H., cited in Hartnett, N., *Notes from his Contemporaries*, p. 116.
8   Smith, 'Closed Circuit', p. 10.
9   Boland, E., 'Closed Circuit', *The Irish Times* (16 April 1971), p. 12.
10 Jordan, J., 'Magazine Scene', *The Irish Press* (29 May 1971), p. 5.
11 Murphy, 'State of the Nation', p. 9.
12 *Ibid.*
13 Murphy, H., Editorial, *Broadsheet*, 11 (*c*. May 1971).
14 Hartnett, Review, *The Irish Times* (17 July 1971), p. 10.
15 Murphy, H., Editorial, *Broadsheet*, 12 (*c*. August 1971).
16 Hartnett, M., Review, *The Irish Times* (9 October 1971), p. 10.
17 Murphy, H., Letter dated 8 December 1977, Hartnett, M., papers, National Library 35,914/8.

18 Murphy, H., Editorial, *Broadsheet*, 13 (1971).

19 Gillespie, E., 'Flogging Culture to the Masses', *The Irish Times* (6 October 1972), p. 10.

20 *Ibid.*

21 Murphy, H., Editorial, *Broadsheet*, 20 (*c.* January 1974).

22 Murphy, H., Editorial, *Broadsheet*, 21 (June 1974).

23 Lynch, Editorial, *The Holy Door*, 2.

24 Hartnett, M., 'Sound and Fury', *Hibernia* (30 May 1975), p. 23.

25 Hartnett, 'Closed Circuit', p. 12.

26 Hartnett, M., 'Handwritten', *The Irish Times* (11 January 1972), p. 8.

27 Hartnett, M., 'Ledwidge', *The Irish Times* (8 April 1972), p. 10.

28 O'Driscoll, D., 'Troubled Thoughts: Poetry Politics in Contemporary Ireland', *Southern Review* (Summer 1995), p. 639.

29 O'Driscoll, D., 'Irish Round-up', *Poetry Review*, 79 (1989) pp. 38–40.

30 Montague, J., *The Figure in the Cave* (1989), pp. 53f.

31 Gillespie, 'Flogging Culture to the Masses', p. 10.

32 Smith, M., 'Irish Poetry since Yeats', *Denver Quarterly* (Winter 1971), p. 24.

33 Smith, M., 'The Contemporary Situation in Irish Poetry', in Dunn, D. (ed.), *Two Decades of Irish Writing* (Cheadle, Carcanet Press, 1975), pp. 162f.

34 Rushe, D., 'Tatler's Parade', *Irish Independent* (12 February 1975), p. 5.

II. '*TÁIMSE* FLABBERGASTED'

1 Smith, N., 'US Professor's strong Plea for Irish Language', *Irish Independent* (3 February 1969), p. 10.

2 '50,000 Dollars for Writing', *The Irish Press* (21 September 1972), p. 3.

3 Kennelly, B., Letter dated 12 September 1972, Hartnett, M., papers, National Library 35,914/6.

4 McLaughlin, 'The Terrier Poet at Home on the Hillside', p. 9.

5 Gillespie, 'Michael Hartnett', p. 10.

6 *Ibid.*

7 *Ibid.*

8 'An Irishman's Diary', *The Irish Times* (2 July 1975), p. 11.

9 Hartnett, M., papers, National Library 35,910/1.

10 Ó Canainn, T., *Seán Ó Riada: His Life and Work* (Cork, Collins Press, 2003), p. 142.

11 Hartnett, M., *The Irish Times* (20 April 1977), p. 8.

12 Harris, B. and Freyer, G. (eds), *Integrating Tradition: The Achievement of Seán Ó Riada* (Ballina, Irish Humanities Centre, 1981), p. 151.

13 Ó Dúill, G., 'The Language Shift', *Poetry Ireland Review*, 80 (2004), p. 95.

14 Ó Tuairisc, E., 'Psychic Partition', *Irish Pages*, 1, 2 (Autumn-Winter, 2002/2003), p. 171.

15 *Ibid.*, pp. 171f.

16 *Ibid.*

17 *Ibid.*

18 *Ibid.*

19 *Ibid.*, pp. 189–194.

20 *Ibid.*

21 *Ibid.*

22 Ó Conaire, B., 'Flann O'Brien: *An Béal Bocht* and other Irish Matters', *Irish University Review*, 3, 2 (Autumn, 1973), p. 122.

23 Hartnett, 'Why Write in Irish?', p. 8.

24 *Ibid.*

25 *Ibid.*

26 *Ibid.*

27 Hartnett, 'Watching our Language', p. 8.

12. 'TO KILL A LANGUAGE IS TO KILL A PEOPLE'

1   Brown, T., *Ireland: A Social and Cultural History 1922–1985* (London, Fontana, 1990), p. 268.

2   Ó Tuathaigh, G., 'Watching our Language', *The Irish Times* (19 April 1977), p. 8.

3   O'Driscoll, Interview, p. 145.

4   Hartnett, 'Why Write in Irish?', p. 8.

5   *Ibid.*

6   'An Irishman's Diary', *The Irish Times* (4 July 1966), p. 7.

7   O'Driscoll, Interview, pp. 140–142.

8   'Tribalism said to be dominant in North', *The Irish Times* (23 February 1974), p. 10.

9   'Policy Reform for Irish on RTÉ', *The Irish Times* (25 February 1974), pp. 1 & 13.

10 Walsh, D., 'Dr O'Brien and the Language', *The Irish Times* (2 April 1975), p. 16.

11 *Ibid.*

12 Rushe, D., 'Tatler's Parade', *Irish Independent* (28 October 1975), p. 10.

13 O'Brien, C. C., 'Pride in the Language', *Irish Independent* (11 May 1991), p. 10.

14 Durcan, 'Hartnett's Farewell', in Montague, *The Poet's Chair*, p. 200.

15 *Ibid.*, p. 211.
16 Hartnett, 'Why Write in Irish?', p. 8.
17 *Ibid.*
18 *Ibid.*
19 Rushe, 'Tatler's Parade', (12 February 1975), p. 5.
20 Hartnett, M., papers, National Library 35,910/1.
21 Ní Ghairbí, R., 'Michael Hartnett's *Adharca Broic*', in McDonagh and Newman, *Remembering Michael Hartnett*, p. 56.
22 Hutchinson, P., *The Frost is all over* (Dublin, The Gallery Press, 1975), pp. 42f.
23 Hartnett, 'Why Write in Irish?', p. 8.

13. 'THE CLINGING BLOOD UPON THE STONES'

1 Kiberd, D., 'The Double Vision of Michael Hartnett', in McDonagh and Newman, *Remembering Michael Hartnett*, p. 33.
2 Fauchereau, S., 'Ecrivains Irlandais', *Les Lettres Nouvelles*, Numero Special (1973), p. 202.
3 Jordan, J., 'Poets and Violence', *Hibernia* (13 July 1973), p. 11.
4 Hartnett, M., 'The new British Poets', *The Irish Press* (25 September 1971), p. 12.
5 Hartnett, 'A Visit to Castletown House', *Collected Poems* (2001) p. 137.
6 Kinsella, T., *Prose Occasions* (Manchester, Carcanet Press, 2009), p. 31.
7 *Ibid.*, pp. 31f.
8 Hartnett, 'Who Killed Bobby Sands', *A Book of Strays*, p. 18.
9 Hartnett, M., 'The Development of Desmond Egan, Poet', *The Irish Press* (5 April 1985), p. 7.
10 Hartnett, 'USA', *Collected Poems* (2001) p. 122.
11 O'Driscoll, Interview, p. 140.
12 *Ibid.*, p. 147.
13 Gregory, A., 'A rebel act', in McDonagh and Newman, *Remembering Michael Hartnett*, p. 135.
14 Denman, P., 'Peter Fallon and the Gallery Press', *Poetry Ireland Review*, 34 (Spring 1992), p. 32.
15 *Ibid.*
16 McFadden, H., 'Packed House for Hartnett Reading', *The Irish Press* (13 March 1975), p. 7.
17 *Ibid.*
18 Collins, D., 'Hartnett's Long Farewell', *St Stephens*, 3, 3 (1976), p. 27.
19 Hartnett, M., cover blurb, *The Retreat of Ita Cagney/Cúlú Íde* (1975).

20 Sealy, D., 'Bilingual', *The Irish Times* (6 March 1976), p. 8.

21 Jordan, J., Review, *Irish Independent* (3 February 1979), p. 7.

22 Gillespie, 'Michael Hartnett', p. 10.

14. 'A LONG WAY TO COME FOR NOTHING'

1 Young, A., *The Niagara Magazine*, 3 (Summer 1975), p. 12.

2 Gillespie, 'Michael Hartnett', p. 10.

3 Carson, C., 'Au revoir', *The Honest Ulsterman*, 50 (Winter 1975), p. 187.

4 *Ibid.*

5 *Ibid.*

6 *Ibid.*

7 *Ibid.*, p. 189.

8 Hartnett, M., Review, *The Irish Times* (14 June 1975), p. 10.

9 Ní Chuilleanáin, E., *Cyphers*, 3 (Summer 1976), p. 42.

10 Collins, 'Hartnett's Long Farewell', p. 27.

11 *Ibid.*, pp. 27f.

12 Durcan, 'The Achievement of Michael Hartnett', p. 5.

13 Hartnett, M., *A Farewell to English* (Dublin, The Gallery Press, 1975), p. 30.

14 *Ibid.*, p. 31.

15 *Ibid.*, p. 32.

16 Hartnett, M., Review, *The Irish Times* (20 July 1971), p. 9.

17 Hartnett, M., Review, *The Irish Times* (23 February 1971), p. 11.

18 Hartnett, M., Review, *The Irish Times* (12 June 1971), p. 10.

19 Hartnett, M., Review, 'Selected Poems of James Clarence Mangan', *Dublin Magazine* (Spring/Summer 1974), p. 118.

20 *The Irish Times* (5 February 1970), p. 14.

21 Hartnett, M., Review, *The Irish Times* (22 May 1971), p. 10.

22 Hartnett, *A Farewell to English*, pp. 32–33.

23 *Ibid.*, p. 33.

24 *Ibid.*, p. 34.

25 *Ibid.*, p. 35.

26 *Ibid.*, p. 28.

27 *Ibid.*

28 *Ibid.*, p. 27.

29 O'Driscoll, Interview, p. 140.

30 Hartnett, *A Farewell to English*, p. 29.

31 Rushe, 'Tatler's Parade', (12 February 1975), p. 5.

32 Carson, 'Au revoir', p. 187.

33 Heaney, S., in Duffy and Dorgan, *Watching the River Flow*, pp. 161f.

34 Grennan, *Facing the Music*, p. 302.

35 *Ibid.*, pp. 305f.

36 Grennan, E., Review, *Irish University Review*, 8, 1 (Spring 1978), p. 117.

37 Sealy, D., 'Back to the Earth', *The Irish Times* (5 July 1975), p. 10.

38 Jordan, J., Review, *Irish Independent* (19 November 1977), p. 12.

39 Marcus, P., Review, *The Irish Press* (31 January 1976), p. 6.

40 Rosenstock, G., 'Faithful and rebellious', *Irish Independent* (14 June 1975), p. 8.

41 *A Necklace of Wrens.*

42 'Poet on the Move', *The Kerryman* (25 July 1975), p. 7.

15. 'No Totems, no Gods'

1   Leland, M., Radio review, *The Irish Times* (15 July 1975), p. 8.

2   *A Necklace of Wrens.*

3   *Ibid.*

4   McLaughlin, 'The Terrier Poet at Home on the Hillside', p. 9.

5   Rosemary Hartnett, correspondence with the author.

6   Fitzmaurice, G., 'An exile out foreign in "Glantine"', in McDonagh and Newman, *Remembering Michael Hartnett*, p. 106.

7   Wheatley, D., 'The Language Issue', *Metre*, 11 (2001), p. 175.

8   Hartnett, M., 'Radio', *Hibernia* (22 July 1977), p. 20.

9   McLaughlin, B., 'Village of the Bodhráns welcomes the President', *The Irish Press* (30 May 1977), p. 7.

10 *Ibid.*

11 Hartnett, M., 'Radio', *Hibernia* (18 February 1977), p. 27.

12 Hartnett, M., 'Radio', *Hibernia* (19 November 1976), p. 25.

13 *Ibid.*

14 Hartnett, 'Radio', (18 February 1977), p. 27.

15 *Ibid.*

16 McLaughlin, 'The Terrier Poet at Home on the Hillside', p. 9.

17 Ní Dhomhnaill, N., cited in Hartnett, N., *Notes from his Contemporaries*, p. 46.

18 'Michael Hartnett in Limerick', in Wylie, D., *32 Counties: Photographs of Ireland* (London, Secker & Warburg, 1989), pp. 33–36.

19 Fallon, P., Letter, Hartnett, M., papers, National Library 35,913/9.

20 *Ibid.*

21 *Ibid.*

22 Miller, L., Letter, Hartnett, M., papers, National Library 35,913/5.

23 Hartnett, M., Cover blurb, *Prisoners* (1977).

24 Durcan, P., Letter, Hartnett, M., papers, National Library 35,913/6.

25 Lysaght, S., 'Michael Hartnett: An Appreciation', *Poetry Ireland Review*, 64 (Spring, 2000), pp. 6–9.

26 De Paor, L., 'Michael Ó hAirtneide's Collected Poems', in McDonagh and Newman, *Remembering Michael Hartnett*, pp. 69f.

27 Jordan, Review (19 November 1977), p. 12.

28 Hartnett, M., papers, National Library 35,910/4(4).

29 Hartnett, 'Radio', (18 February 1977), p. 27.

16. 'A Conspiracy of One'

1 McLaughlin, 'The Terrier Poet at Home on the Hillside', p. 9.

2 McLaughlin, B., 'How the News travels', *The Irish Press* (7 December 1978), p. 11.

3 Jordan, J., 'Magazine Scene', *The Irish Press* (6 April 1978), p. 6.

4 McLaughlin, 'The Terrier Poet at Home on the Hillside', p. 9.

5 *Ibid.*

6 Rosemary Hartnett, correspondence with the author.

7 Ní Ghairbí, R., 'Michael Hartnett's *Adharca Broic*', in McDonagh and Newman, *Remembering Michael Hartnett*, p. 55.

8 O'Driscoll, D., Review, *Hibernia* (6 September 1979), p. 16.

9 De Paor, L., 'Michael Ó hAirtneide's Collected Poems' in McDonagh and Newman, *Remembering Michael Hartnett*, p. 69.

10 *Ibid.*, p. 68.

11 *Ibid.*

12 Hartnett, M., papers, National Library 35,925.

13 Rosemary Hartnett, correspondence with the author.

14 Ní Dhomhnaill, N., in Hartnett, N., *Notes from his Contemporaries*, p. 45.

15 *Ibid.*, p. 46.

16 Ní Dhomhnaill, N., 'Foighne Crainn: The patience of a Tree', *Metre*, 11 (2001), pp. 151f.

17 Ní Dhomhnaill, N., in Hartnett, N., *Notes from his Contemporaries*, p. 44.

18 *Ibid.*, p. 46.

19 *Ibid.*

20 Ní Dhomhnaill, 'Foighne Crainn', p. 152.

21 MacAmhlaigh, D., *The Irish Press* (6 July 1979), p. 8.

22 O'Driscoll, D., Review, *Hibernia* (4 January 1979), p. 10.

23 Ó Dúill, G., 'The Language Shift', p. 96.

24 Hartnett, M., papers, National Library 35,913/9–10.

25 Leland, M., Review, *The Irish Times* (25 October 1976), p. 8.

26 Leland, M., Review, *The Irish Times* (31 December 1979), p. 8.

27 Lappin, M., Radio review, *The Irish Press* (3 February 1979), p. 8.

28 Lappin, M., Radio review, *The Irish Press* (20 October 1979) p. 8.

29 Lappin, M., Radio review, *The Irish Press* (4 October 1980), p. 8.

30 Leland, M., Review, *The Irish Times* (20 October 1980), p. 8.

31 Lappin, Radio review (4 October 1980), p. 8.

32 Fitzmaurice, G., 'An exile out foreign in "Glantine"', in McDonagh and Newman, *Remembering Michael Hartnett*, p. 106.

33 Buckley, V., *Memory Ireland* (New York, Penguin Books, 1985), pp. 226–229.

34 *Ibid.*

35 Fitzmaurice, G., 'An exile out foreign in "Glantine"', in McDonagh and Newman, *Remembering Michael Hartnett*, p. 104.

36 Hartnett, M., 'Féintrua', *Do Nuala: Foighne Chrainn* (Dublin, Coiscéim, 1984), pp. 22–23.

37 O'Driscoll, Interview, pp. 140–142.

38 Hartnett, M., 'The Purge', *The Flowering Tree* (Dublin, Wolfhound Press, 1991), p. 179.

39 *A Necklace of Wrens.*

40 Hartnett, M., 'Radio', *Hibernia* (22 October 1976), p. 28.

41 Titley, A., 'Innti and onward', in Dorgan, T., *Irish Poetry since Kavanagh* (Dublin, Four Courts Press, 1996), p. 94.

42 Titley, A., in Bolger, D. (ed.), *The Bright Wave* (Dublin, Raven Arts Press, 1986), p. 21.

43 Deane, J. F., Review, *Books Ireland* (September 1984), p. 155.

44 *Ibid.*

45 Kennelly, B., Review, *Poetry Ireland Review*, 15 (Winter, 1985/1986), p. 26.

46 *Ibid.*

47 *Ibid.*, p. 29.

17. 'POET CAUSES MAYHEM WITH SALAD SAGA'

1 Hartnett, M., *Maiden Street Ballad* (Limerick, Observer Press, 1980), p. 3.

2 *Ibid.*, p. 60.

3 Hartnett, M., 'Radio', *Hibernia* (7 January 1977), p. 35.

4 Byrnes, M., 'Poet causes Mayhem with Salad Saga', *The Limerick Echo* (6 August 1983), p. 1.

5 Hartnett, M., papers, National Library 35,910/3.

6 'Michael believes in Workshops', *The Kerryman* (10 June 1983), p. 9.

7 Smith, N., 'Mother of Two "Aunt" to 4,000 Alcan Workers', *Irish*

Independent (22 April 1982), p. 9.

8   *A Necklace of Wrens.*

9   Hartnett, 'That Actor Kiss', *Collected Poems* (2001) p. 212.

18. 'MY ENGLISH DAM BURSTS'

1   Rosemary Hartnett, correspondence with the author.

2   Hartnett, M., ' Somewhere in France', *Poems to Younger Women* (Oldcastle, The Gallery Press, 1988), p. 14.

3   Hartnett, 'Inchicore Haiku', *Collected Poems* (2001), pp. 148–165.

4   Bolger, D. in Hartnett, N., *Notes from his Contemporaries*, p. 16.

5   Curtis, 'A Life in Poetry', p. 164.

6   Dawe, G., 'Bringing Poetry down to Earth', *Sunday Independent* (2 December 1984), p. 188.

7   Hartnett, 'Inchicore Haiku', *Collected Poems* (2001), pp. 148–165.

8   *Ibid.*

9   *Ibid.*

10   Hartnett, M., papers, National Library 35,888/3.

11   *Ibid.*

12   Sirr, P., 'The Short and the Long', *The Irish Times* (21 September 1985), p. 11.

13   Grennan, E., 'Poet and Translator', *The Irish Times* (18 October 1986), p. 25.

14   Hartnett, M., papers, National Library 35,889/9.

19. 'THE BIBLE IN SCOUSE'

1   Bolger, D., in Hartnett, N., *Notes from his Contemporaries*, p. 16.

2   Hartnett, 'Angela Liston', *A Book of Strays*, p. 57.

3   Hartnett, M., 'Wrestling with Ó Bruadair', in MacReamoinn, *The Pleasures of Gaelic Poetry*, p. 66.

4   Hartnett, M., papers, National Library 35,889.

5   Hartnett, M., 'Wrestling with Ó Bruadair', in MacReamoinn, *The Pleasures of Gaelic Poetry*, p. 66.

6   Agee, C., 'A Dying Order set in Amber', *Fortnight*, 247 (January 1987), p. 22.

7   Hartnett, M., 'Wrestling with Ó Bruadair', in MacReamoinn, *The Pleasures of Gaelic Poetry*, p. 78.

8   Hartnett, M., *Ó Bruadair* (Dublin, The Gallery Press, 1985), p. 15.

9   O'Grady, T., '(Re)Visiting Michael Hartnett', *Irish Literary Supplement*, 9, 1 (2000), p. 27.

10 Hartnett, M., 'To see the Art of Poetry lost', *Ó Bruadair* (1985), p. 27.

11 O'Grady, T., 'Lines of Descent', *Compost*, 7 (Spring 1996), p. 32.

12 Hartnett, M., papers, National Library 35,914/6.

13 Hartnett, M., 'Wrestling with Ó Bruadair', in MacReamoinn, *The Pleasures of Gaelic Poetry*, p. 72.

14 Hartnett, M., 'Poets and Translators', *The Irish Times* (6 November 1975), p. 8.

15 Mac Erlean, J., cited in Hartnett, M., papers, National Library, 35/889.

16 Hartnett, M., papers, National Library 35/889.

17 Deane, J. F., Review, *Sunday Independent* (9 February 1986), p. 14.

18 Ellis, C., 'Wit and Crispness', *Books Ireland* (September 1986), p. 168.

19 O'Driscoll, Interview, pp. 139–147.

20 White, 'Heartbreak in Two Languages', p. 8.

20. 'A RIVER OF TEARS'

1 Grennan, E., *Facing the Music*, p. 300.

2 Bolger, D., in Hartnett, N., *Notes from his Contemporaries*, p. 16.

3 O'Driscoll, Interview, p. 147.

4 Fallon, P., Letter dated 23 August 1988, Michael Hartnett papers, National Library 35,913/9.

5 Bolger, D., Undated Letter, Michael Hartnett papers, National Library 35,915/3.

6 Hartnett, R., Letter dated 2 September 1988, Michael Hartnett papers, National Library 35,920.

7 Bolger, D., Letter dated 12 August 1992, Michael Hartnett papers, National Library, 35,913/3.

8 White, 'Heartbreak in Two Languages', p. 14.

9 *Ibid.*

10 *Ibid.*

11 O'Driscoll, Interview, p. 145.

12 Hartnett, M., papers, National Library 35,910/3.

13 Hartnett, M., papers, National Library 35,910.

14 *Ibid.*

15 *Ibid.*

16 Hartnett, 'For All the Children', *A Book of Strays*, p. 58.

21. 'HEARTBREAK IN TWO LANGUAGES'

1 White, 'Heartbreak in Two Languages', p. 8.

2   O'Driscoll, Interview, p. 147.

3   *Ibid.*, pp. 140–142.

4   Fallon, P., 'An Afterword', in Hartnett, M., *Translations* (Oldcastle, The Gallery Press, 2003), p. 126.

5   Smith, 'Remembering Michael Hartnett', p. 12.

6   Grennan, *Facing the Music*, p. 299.

7   Hartnett, M., papers, National Library 35,910/1.

8   Heaney, S., in McDonagh and Newman, *Remembering Michael Hartnett*, p. 12.

9   Dorgan, T., *Sunday Independent* (17 October 1999), p. 14.

10 O'Grady, '(Re)Visiting Michael Hartnett', p. 27.

11 Hartnett, M., *Ó Bruadair* (1985), pp. 14f.

12 Hartnett, 'Poets and Translators', p. 8.

13 Hartnett, M., in Haicéad, P. and Hartnett, M., *Haicéad* (Oldcastle, The Gallery Press, 1993).

14 Sealy, D., Review, *Poetry Ireland Review*, 45 (Spring 1995), p. 76.

15 Lysaght, 'Michael Hartnett: An Appreciation', p. 8.

16 Rosenstock, G., 'The unique Beauty of Hartnett's *Tao*', in McDonagh and Newman, *Remembering Michael Hartnett*, p. 45.

17 Rosenstock, G., 'Some Fury little Sound', *Poetry Ireland Review*, 62 (Autumn, 1999), pp. 111–113.

18 Traynor, D., 'The Economy of Maturity', *Books Ireland* (May 1999), p. 140.

19 Mhac an tSaoi, M., 'Writing in Modern Irish', *Southern Review* (Summer 1995), p. 427.

20 Mhac an tSaoi, M., 'The Clerisy and the Folk', *Poetry Ireland Review* (Winter 1988), p. 34.

22. 'ALCOHOL'S A CUNNING BEAST'

1   Hartnett, 'Sibelius in Silence', *Collected Poems* (2001), p. 226.

2   Curtis, 'A Life in Poetry', p. 166.

3   Keane, J. B., Letter dated 14 February 1990, Hartnett M., papers, National Library 35,914/4.

4   Durcan, in Montague, *The Poet's Chair*, p. 218.

5   *A Necklace of Wrens.*

6   Durcan, in Montague, *The Poet's Chair*, pp. 197f.

7   Curtis, 'A Life in Poetry', p. 164.

8   O'Driscoll, Interview, p. 147.

9   White, 'Heartbreak in Two Languages', p. 8.

10 Hartnett, M., papers, National Library 35,910/3.

11 Dwyer Hickey, C., in Hartnett, N., *Notes from his Contemporaries*, p. 74.

12 Ní Dhomhnaill, N., in Hartnett, N., *Notes from his Contemporaries*, p. 47.

13 Ní Dhomhnaill, N., 'Foighne Crainn', p. 148.

14 Ní Dhomhnaill, N., in Hartnett, N., *Notes from his Contemporaries*, p. 47.

15 Lynch, *Parson's Bookshop*, p. 202.

16 Bolger, D., in Hartnett, N., *Notes from his Contemporaries*, p. 16.

17 *Ibid*.

18 Hartnett, M., papers, National Library 35,944/3.

19 Hartnett, 'Parables for Clane', *A Book of Strays*, p. 53.

20 Ní Dhomhnaill, N., in Hartnett, N., *Notes from his Contemporaries*, p. 47.

21 Smith, M., 'Remembering Michael Hartnett'.

22 McLaughlin, B., 'Hunting the Hartnett', *Sunday Independent* (26 February 1995), p. 12.

23 McLaughlin, B., 'In love with the Pagan Irish Heart', *Sunday Independent* (26 December 1999), p. 11.

24 O'Brien, P., in Hartnett, N., *Notes from his Contemporaries*, p. 20.

25 Durcan, in Montague, *The Poet's Chair*, p. 199.

26 *Ibid*., p. 200.

27 Johnston, F., 'Treading the Wine Press', *Books Ireland* (Summer 2001), p. 180.

28 *Ibid*.

29 Ní Dhomhnaill, N., in Hartnett, N., *Notes from his Contemporaries*, p. 49.

30 Hartnett, M., Review, *The Irish Times* (20 November 1971), p. 10.

31 Curtis, 'A Life in Poetry', p. 170.

32 Liddy, *The Doctor's House*, p. 84.

33 Bolger, D., in Hartnett, N., *Notes from his Contemporaries*, p. 17.

CONCLUSION

1   Heaney, S., in McDonagh and Newman, *Remembering Michael Hartnett*, p. 13.

2   Grennan, *Facing the Music*, p. 299.

3   *A Necklace of Wrens*.

4   Hartnett, *A Farewell to English*, p. 33.

Bibliography

Agee, C., 'A dying Order set in Amber', *Fortnight*, 247 (January 1987), p. 22

Arena, 3, Editorial (Summer 1964), p. 1

Arena, 4, Editorial (Spring 1965), p. 1

Armstrong, J., 'A new Force in Irish Poetry Publishing', *The Irish Times* (27 January 1972)

Bardwell, L., *A Restless Life* (Dublin, Liberties Press, 2008)

Begnal, M. S. (ed.), *Honeysuckle, Honeyjuice: A Tribute to James Liddy* (Galway, Arlen House, 2006)

Boland, E., 'The Poet facing Both Ways', *The Irish Times* (29 January 1971)

Boland, E., 'Poetry Reading at Project Art Centre', *The Irish Times* (2 August 1971)

Boland, E., 'Closed Circuit', *The Irish Times* (16 April 1971)

Boland, J., 'Poetry', *The Irish Press* (15 February 1972)

Bolger, D. (ed.), *The Bright Wave* (Dublin, Raven Arts Press, 1986)

Brennan, R., Review, *Books Ireland* (September 2003), p. 200

Brown, T., *Ireland: A Social and Cultural History* (London, Fontana, 1990)

Buckley, V., *Memory Ireland* (New York, Penguin Books, 1985)

Byrnes, M., 'Poet causes Mayhem with Salad Saga', *The Limerick Echo* (6 August 1983), p. 1

Carson, C., 'Au revoir', *The Honest Ulsterman*, 50 (Winter 1975), p. 187

Clarke, R. D. (ed.), *Austin Clarke remembered* (Dublin, Bridge Press, 1996)

Clyde, T., *Irish Literary Magazines: An Outline History and Descriptive Bibliography* (Dublin, Irish Academic Press, 2003)

Collins, D., 'Hartnett's Long Farewell', *St Stephens*, 3, 3 (1976), p. 27

Corcoran, N., *Poets of Modern Ireland* (Carbondale, Southern Illinois University Press, 1999)

Coughlan, P. and Davis, A. (eds), *Modernism and Ireland: The Poetry of the 1930s* (Cork, Cork University Press, 1995)

Curtis, T., 'A Life in Poetry', *Metre*, 11 (Dublin, Lilliput Press, 2001), p. 166

Dawe, G., 'Bringing Poetry down to Earth', *Sunday Independent* (2 December 1984)

Deane, J. F., Review, *Books Ireland* (September 1984), p. 155

Deane, J. F., Review, *Sunday Independent* (9 February 1986)

Denman, P., 'Peter Fallon and the Gallery Press', *Poetry Ireland Review*, 34 (Spring 1992), p. 32

Dorgan, T. (ed.), *Irish Poetry since Kavanagh* (Dublin, Four Courts Press, 1996)

Dorgan, T., *Sunday Independent* (17 October 1999)

Duffy, N. and Dorgan, T. (eds), *Watching the River Flow: A Century in Irish Poetry* (Dublin, *Poetry Ireland*, 1999)

Dunn, D. (ed.), *Two Decades of Irish Writing* (Cheadle, Carcanet, 1975)

Durcan, P., 'The Achievement of Michael Hartnett', *The Cork Examiner* (27 February 1978)

Durcan, P., *Daddy, Daddy* (Belfast, Blackstaff Press, 1990)

Durcan, P., *The Poet's Chair* (Dublin, Lilliput Press, 2008)

Egan, D. and Hartnett, M. (eds), *Choice* (Dublin, Goldsmith Press, 1973)

Ellis, C., 'Wit and Crispness', *Books Ireland* (September 1986), p. 168

Fauchereau, S., 'Ecrivains Irlandais', *Les Lettres Nouvelles*, Numero Special (1973), p. 202

Fennell, D., 'Welcome to the *Arena*', *The Irish Press* (27 May 1963)

Foley, D., 'Tea-boy of the Western World', *Sunday Review* (23 July 1961)

Gillespie, E., 'Flogging Culture to the Masses', *The Irish Times* (6 October 1972)

Gillespie, E., 'Michael Hartnett', *The Irish Times* (5 March 1975)

Goodby, J., *Irish Poetry since 1950* (Manchester, Manchester University Press, 2000)

Grennan, E., Review, *Irish University Review*, 8, 1 (Spring 1978), p. 117

Grennan, E., 'Poet and Translator', *The Irish Times* (18 October 1986)

Grennan, E., *Facing the Music: Irish Poetry in the Twentieth Century* (Omaha, Creighton University Press, 1999)

Haicéad, P. and Hartnett, M., *Haicéad* (Oldcastle, The Gallery Press, 1993)

Harris, B. and Freyer, G. (eds), *Integrating Tradition, The Achievement of Seán Ó Riada* (Ballina, Irish Humanities Centre, 1981)

Hartnett, M., papers, National Library of Ireland, 35,875–35,909

Hartnett, M., papers, National Library of Ireland, 35,910–35,912

Hartnett, M., papers, National Library of Ireland, 35,913–35,915

Hartnett, M., papers, National Library of Ireland, 35,916–35,928

Hartnett, M., *Anatomy of a Cliché* (Dublin, The Dolmen Press, 1968)

Hartnett, M., 'Poet's Progress', *The Irish Times* (11 November 1968)

Hartnett, M., 'London and the Emigrant Stint', *The Irish Times* (12 November 1968)

Hartnett, M., 'The Dublin Literary World', *The Irish Times* (13 November 1968)

Hartnett, M., 'The Town the Young leave', *The Irish Times* (10 June 1969)

Hartnett, M., *The Hag of Beare* (Dublin New Writers' Press, 1969)

Hartnett, M., *Selected Poems* (Dublin, New Writers' Press, 1970)

Hartnett, M., Review, *Hibernia* (18 December 1970), p. 12

Hartnett, M., Review, *The Irish Times* (23 February 1971)

Hartnett, M., 'Closed Circuit', *The Irish Times* (23 April 1971)

Hartnett, M., Review, *The Irish Times* (22 May 1971)

Hartnett, M., Review, *The Irish Times* (12 June 1971)

Hartnett, M., Review, *The Irish Times* (17 July 1971)

Hartnett, M., Review, *The Irish Times* (20 July 1971)

Hartnett, M., 'The new British Poets', *The Irish Press* (25 September 1971)

Hartnett, M., Review, *The Irish Times* (9 October 1971)

Hartnett, M., Review, *The Irish Times* (20 November 1971)

Hartnett, M., 'Handwritten', *The Irish Times* (11 January 1972)

Hartnett, M., 'Ledwidge', *The Irish Times* (8 April 1972)

Hartnett, M., Letters, *The Irish Times* (27 June 1972)

Hartnett, M., *Tao* (Dublin, New Writers' Press, 1972)

Hartnett, M., *Gypsy Ballads* (Dublin, Goldsmith Press 1973)

Hartnett, M., Review, 'Selected Poems of James Clarence Mangan', *Dublin Magazine* (Spring/Summer 1974), p. 118

Hartnett, M., 'Sound and Fury', *Hibernia* (30 May 1975), p. 23

Hartnett, M., Review, *The Irish Times* (14 June 1975)

Hartnett, M., 'Why Write in Irish?' *The Irish Times* (26 August 1975)

Hartnett, M., 'Poets and Translators', *The Irish Times* (6 November 1975)

Hartnett, M., *A Farewell to English* (Dublin, The Gallery Press, 1975)

Hartnett, M., *The Retreat of Ita Cagney/Cúlú Íde* (Kildare, Goldsmith Press, 1975).

Hartnett, M., 'Radio', *Hibernia* (22 October 1976), p. 28

Hartnett, M., 'Radio', *Hibernia* (19 November 1976), p. 25

Hartnett, M., 'Radio', *Hibernia* (7 January 1977), p. 35

Hartnett, M., 'Radio', *Hibernia* (17 January 1977), p. 35

Hartnett, M., 'Radio', *Hibernia* (18 February 1977), p. 27

Hartnett, M., 'Watching our Language', *The Irish Times* (20 April 1977)

Hartnett, M., 'Radio', *Hibernia* (29 April 1977), p. 29

Hartnett, M., 'Radio', *Hibernia* (22 July 1977), p. 20

Hartnett, M., *Poems in English* (Dublin, The Dolmen Press, 1977)

Hartnett, M., *Prisoners* (Old Deerfield, Deerfield Press, and Dublin, The Gallery Press, 1977)

Hartnett, M., *Adharca Broic* (Dublin, The Gallery Press, 1978)

Hartnett, M., *A Farewell to English* (enlarged edition; Dublin, The Gallery Press, 1975)

Hartnett, M., *Maiden Street Ballad* (Limerick, Observer Press, 1980)

Hartnett, M., *This was Arena* (Naas, The Malton Press, 1982)

Hartnett, M., *An Phurgóid* (Dublin, Coiscéim, 1983)

Hartnett, M., *Do Nuala: Foighne Chrainn* (Dublin, Coiscéim, 1984)

Hartnett, M., *Collected Poems*, Volume 1 (Dublin, Raven Arts Press, 1984)

Hartnett, M., 'Christmas in Newcastle West', *Old Limerick Journal*, 17 (Winter 1984)

Hartnett, M., 'The Development of Desmond Egan, Poet', *The Irish Press* (5 April 1985)

Hartnett, M., *Inchicore Haiku* (Dublin, Raven Arts Press, 1985)

Hartnett, M., *Ó Bruadair* (Dublin, The Gallery Press, 1985)

Hartnett, M., *A Necklace of Wrens* (Dublin, The Gallery Press, 1987)

Hartnett, M., *Poems to Younger Women* (Dublin, The Gallery Press, 1988)

Hartnett, M., *Dánta Naomh Eoin na Crois* (Dublin, Coiscéim, 1991)

Hartnett, M., *The Flowering Tree* (Dublin, Wolfhound Press, 1991)

Hartnett, M., *The Killing of Dreams* (Oldcastle, The Gallery Press, 1992)

Hartnett, M., *Haicéad* (Oldcastle, The Gallery Press, 1993)

Hartnett, M., *Selected and New Poems* (Oldcastle, The Gallery Press, 1994)

Hartnett, M., *Ó Rathaille: The Poems of Aodhaghán Ó Rathaille* (Oldcastle, The Gallery Press, 1998)

Hartnett, M., *Collected Poems* (Oldcastle, The Gallery Press, 2001)

Hartnett, M., *A Book of Strays* (Oldcastle, The Gallery Press, 2002)

Hartnett, M., *Translations* (Oldcastle, The Gallery Press, 2003)

Hartnett, M. and Ryan, R., Letters, *The Irish Times* (23 June 1972)

Hartnett, N. (ed.), *Notes from his Contemporaries: A Tribute to Michael Hart-*

nett (Lulu, 2010)

Hutchinson, P., *The Frost is all over* (Dublin, The Gallery Press, 1975)

The Irish Press, '50,000 Dollars for Writing' (21 September 1972)

The Irish Times, 'An Irishman's Diary' (4 July 1966)

The Irish Times, 'An Irishman's Diary' (3 August 1968)

The Irish Times, 'The Future of Irish Poetry' (5 February 1970)

The Irish Times, 'The Small Imprints' (6 November 1973)

The Irish Times, 'Tribalism said to be dominant in North' (23 February 1974)

The Irish Times, 'Policy Reform for Irish on RTÉ' (25 February 1974)

The Irish Times, 'An Irishman's Diary' (2 July 1975)

Johnston, F., 'Treading the Wine Press', *Books Ireland* (Summer 2001), p. 180

Jordan, J., papers, National Library of Ireland, 35,041/2

Jordan, J., papers, National Library of Ireland, 35,077

Jordan, J., papers, National Library of Ireland, 35,089

Jordan, J., Editorial, *Poetry Ireland*, 1, 1 (1962)

Jordan, J., *Poetry Ireland*, 3 (Spring 1964), p. 3

Jordan, J., 'Magazine Scene', *The Irish Press* (29 May 1971)

Jordan, J., 'Poets and Violence', *Hibernia* (13 July 1973), p. 11

Jordan, J., Review, *Irish Independent* (19 November 1977)

Jordan, J., 'Magazine Scene', *The Irish Press* (6 April 1978)

Jordan, J., Review, *Irish Independent* (3 February 1979)

Jordan, J., Review, *Cyphers*, 11 (Winter 1979), p. 45

Jordan, J., *Crystal Clear: The Selected Prose of John Jordan* (Dublin, Lilliput Press, 2006)

Joyce, T., *Sole Glum Trek* (Dublin, New Writers' Press, 1967)

Kemmy, J. (ed.), *The Limerick Anthology* (Dublin, Gill & Macmillan, 1996)

Kennelly, B., Review, *Poetry Ireland Review*, 15 (Winter, 1985/1986), p. 26

The Kerryman, 'Poet on the Move' (25 July 1975), p. 7

The Kerryman, 'Michael believes in Workshops' (10 June 1983), p. 9

Kersnowski, F., *The Outsiders – Poets of Contemporary Ireland* (Fort Worth, Texas Christian University Press, 1975)

Kiberd, D. (ed.), *The Flowering Tree: An Crann Faoi Bláth* (Dublin, Wolfhound Press, 1995)

Kilroy, T., 'In memoriam: John Jordan', *Irish Review*, 6 (Spring 1989)

Kinsella, T., *The Dual Tradition* (Manchester, Carcanet Press, 1995)

Kinsella, T., *Prose Occasions* (Manchester, Carcanet Press, 2009)

Lappin, M., Radio review, *The Irish Press* (3 February 1979)

Lappin, M., Radio review, *The Irish Press* (20 October 1979)

Lappin, M., Radio review, *The Irish Press* (4 October 1980)

Leland, M., Radio review, *The Irish Times* (15 July 1975)

Leland, M., Review, *The Irish Times* (25 October 1976)

Leland, M., Review, *The Irish Times* (31 December 1979)

Leland, M., Review, *The Irish Times* (20 October 1980)

Liddy, J., Letter dated 26 February 1963, New Writers' Press Records 1967–1996, National Library of Ireland, 40,136/1

Liddy, J., 'A Poetry Reading', *Kilkenny Magazine* (Spring 1965), p. 35

Liddy, J., Letter dated 1971, National Library, New Writers' Press Records, 40,136/2

Liddy, J., *This Was Arena* (Naas, The Malton Press, 1982)

Liddy, J., *The Doctor's House* (Clare, Salmon Publishing, 2004)

Liddy, J., *The Full Shilling* (Clare, Salmon Publishing, 2009)

Lisker, R., 'Poetry and Literary Pubs', *Hibernia* (24 October 1969), p. 22

Lynch, B., Biographical notes, *The Holy Door*, 2 (Winter 1965), p. 35

Lynch, B., Letters, *The Irish Press* (13 May 1971)

Lynch, B., *Parson's Bookshop* (Dublin, Liffey Press, 2006)

Lysaght, S., 'Michael Hartnett: An Appreciation', *Poetry Ireland Review*, 64 (Spring, 2000), pp. 6–9

Mhac an tSaoi, M., 'The Clerisy and the Folk', *Poetry Ireland Review* (Winter 1988), p. 34

Mhac an tSaoi, M., 'Writing in Modern Irish', *Southern Review* (Summer 1995), p. 427

MacAmhlaigh, D., *The Irish Press* (6 July 1979)

MacReamoinn, S. (ed.), *The Pleasures of Gaelic Poetry* (London, Allen Lane, 1982)

Marcus, P., Review, *The Irish Press* (31 January 1976)

McCafferty, N., 'At the Poetry Recital', *The Irish Times* (9 March 1971)

McDonagh, J. and Newman, S. (eds), *Remembering Michael Hartnett* (Dublin, Four Courts Press, 2006)

McFadden, H., 'Packed House for Hartnett Reading', *The Irish Press* (13 March 1975)

McFadden, H., *Crystal Clear: The Selected Prose of John Jordan* (Dublin, Lilliput Press, 2006)

McGurk, T., 'Spring Poetry', *The Irish Times* (13 May 1972)

McGurk, T., Letters, *The Irish Times* (10 July 1972)

McLaughlin, B., 'Village of the Bodhráns welcomes the President', *The Irish Press* (30 May 1977), p. 7

McLaughlin, B., 'The Terrier Poet at Home on the Hillside', *The Irish Press* (28 September 1978)

McLaughlin, B., 'How the News travels', *The Irish Press* (7 December 1978)

McLaughlin, B., 'Hunting the Hartnett', *Sunday Independent* (26 February 1995)

McLaughlin, B., 'In love with the Pagan Irish Heart', *Sunday Independent* (26 December 1999)

Metre, 11, Winter 2001/2002 (Dublin, published in association with Lilliput Press, 2001)

Montague, J., *The Figure in the Cave* (Dublin, Lilliput Press, 1989)

Montague, J., *Company: A Chosen Life* (London, Duckworth, 2001)

Montague, J. (ed.), *The Poet's Chair* (Dublin, Lilliput Press, 2008)

Morrish, H., *The Poet Speaks* (London, Routledge, 1968)

Murphy, H., 'State of the Nation', *The Irish Times* (9 July 1969)

Murphy, H., Editorial, *Broadsheet*, 11 (*c.* May 1971)

Murphy, H., Editorial, *Broadsheet*, 12 (*c.* August 1971)

Murphy, H., Editorial, *Broadsheet*, 20 (*c.* January 1974)

A Necklace of Wrens [Film], Harvest Films (1999)

Nicholson, R., 'Signatures of all Things I am here to read', *James Joyce Quarterly*, 38, 3–4 (Spring/Summer 2001), p. 294

Ní Chuilleanáin, E., *Cyphers*, 3 (Summer 1976), p. 42

Ní Dhomhnaill, N., *Selected Poems of Nuala Ní Dhomhnaill* [translated by Michael Hartnett] (Dublin, Raven Arts Press, 1986)

Ní Dhomhnaill, N., 'Foighne Crainn: The Patience of a Tree', *Metre*, 11 (Dublin, Lilliput Press, 2001), p. 148

Ní Fhrighil, M., Review, *The Irish Times* (13 March 1973)

O'Brien, A. (ed.), *On the Counterscarp* (Galway, Salmon Publishing, 1991)

O'Brien, C. C., 'Pride in the Language', *Irish Independent* (11 May 1991)

Ó Canainn, T., *Seán Ó Riada: His Life and Work* (Cork, Collins Press, 2003)

Ó Conaire, B., 'Flann O'Brien: *An Béal Bocht* and other Irish Matters', *Irish University Review*, 3, 2 (Autumn 1973), p. 122

O'Driscoll, D., Review, *Hibernia* (6 September 1974), p. 16

O'Driscoll, D., Review, *Hibernia* (4 January 1979), p. 10

O'Driscoll, D., 'Irish Round-up', *Poetry Review*, 79 (1989), pp. 38–40

O'Driscoll, D., 'Troubled Thoughts: Poetry Politics in Contemporary Ireland', *Southern Review* (Summer 1995), p. 639

O'Driscoll, D., Interview, *Metre*, 11 (Dublin, Lilliput Press, 2001), p. 142

Ó Dúill, G., 'The Language Shift', *Poetry Ireland Review*, 80 (2004), p. 95

O'Grady, T., 'Lines of Descent', *Compost*, 7 (Spring 1996), p. 32

O'Grady, T., '(Re)Visiting Michael Hartnett', *Irish Literary Supplement*, 9, 1 (2000), p. 27

O'Riordan, D., *The Irish Times* (31 March 1969)

Ó Tuairisc, E., 'Psychic Partition', *Irish Pages*, 1, 2 (Autumn–Winter, 2002/2003), p. 171

Ó Tuathaigh, G., 'Watching our Language', *The Irish Times* (19 April 1977), p. 8

Quidnunc, 'Irishman's Diary', *The Irish Times* (27 November 1963)

Quidnunc, 'Irishman's Diary', *The Irish Times* (1 April 1969)

Rosenstock, G., 'Faithful and rebellious', *Irish Independent* (14 June 1975)

Rosenstock, G., *Portrait of the Artist as an Abominable Snowman* [translated by Michael Hartnett] (London, Forest Books, 1990)

Rosenstock, G., 'Some Fury little Sound', *Poetry Ireland Review*, 62 (Autumn 1999), pp. 111–113

Rushe, D., 'Tatler's Parade', *Irish Independent* (2 November 1973)

Rushe, D., 'Tatler's Parade', *Irish Independent* (12 February 1975)

Rushe, D., 'Tatler's Parade', *Irish Independent* (28 October 1975)

Scannell, V., 'Craft and Matter', *The Irish Press* (8 May 1971)

Schirmer, G., *Out of What Began: A History of Irish Poetry in English* (Ithaca, Cornell University Press, 1998)

Sealy, D., 'Four Poets' *The Irish Times* (10 August 1968)

Sealy, D., 'Back to the Earth', *The Irish Times* (5 July 1975)

Sealy, D., 'Bilingual', *The Irish Times* (6 March 1976)

Sealy, D., Review, *Poetry Ireland Review*, 45 (Spring 1995), p. 76

Simmons, J., 'New Talent', *Fortnight*, 64 (22 June 1973), p. 18

Simmons, J. (ed.), *Ten Irish Poets* (Cheadle, Carcanet Press, 1974)

Sirr, P., 'The Short and the Long', *The Irish Times* (21 September 1985)

Smith, M., Letter, *The Irish Times* (29 April 1969)

Smith, M., 'Closed Circuit', *The Irish Times* (2 April 1971)

Smith, M., Editorial, *The Lace Curtain*, 4 (Summer 1971), pp. 3f

Smith, M., 'Irish Poetry since Yeats', *Denver Quarterly* (Winter 1971), p. 24

Smith, M. 'John Jordan: Beyond Categories …', *The Irish Times* (14 June 1988)

Smith, M., 'Michael Hartnett: A Memoir', *Metre*, 11 (Dublin, Lilliput Press, 2001), p. 156

Smith, M., 'Remembering Michael Hartnett', *The Irish Times* (16 February 2009)

Smith, M. and Joyce, T., Editorial, *The Lace Curtain*, 2 (Spring 1970)

Smith, N., 'US Professor's strong Plea for Irish Language', *Irish Independent* (3 February 1969)

Smith, N., 'Mother of Two "Aunt" to 4,000 Alcan Workers', *Irish Independent* (22 April 1982)

Sunday Independent, 'From Limerick who writes and writes' (16 September 1962)

Traynor, D., 'The Economy of Maturity', *Books Ireland* (May 1999)

Walsh, D., 'Dr O'Brien and the Language', *The Irish Times* (2 April 1975), p. 16

Wheatley, D., 'The Language Issue', *Metre*, 11 (2001), p. 175

White, V., 'Heartbreak in Two Languages', *The Irish Times* (15 December 1994)

Woods, M., 'Ten years of Irish poetry', *Hibernia* (17 April 1970), p. 20

Woods, M., 'John Jordan 1930–1988', *Poetry Ireland Review*, 25 (Spring, 1989), p. 15

Wylie, D., *32 Counties: Photographs of Ireland* (London, Secker & Warburg, 1989)

Young, A., *The Niagara Magazine*, 3 (Summer 1975), p. 12

INDEX